Mozart &
Beethoven

THE CONCEPT OF LOVE
IN THEIR OPERAS

BOOKS BY IRVING SINGER

Mozart & Beethoven: The Concept of Love in Their Operas with new preface, The Irving Singer Library

Meaning in Life trilogy with new prefaces, The Irving Singer Library

The Nature of Love trilogy with new prefaces, The Irving Singer Library

Philosophy of Love: A Partial Summing-Up

Cinematic Mythmaking: Philosophy in Film

Ingmar Bergman, Cinematic Philosopher: Reflections on His Creativity

Three Philosophical Filmmakers: Hitchcock, Welles, Renoir

Sex: A Philosophical Primer, expanded edition

Feeling and Imagination: The Vibrant Flux of Our Existence

Explorations in Love and Sex

Sex: A Philosophical Primer

George Santayana, Literary Philosopher

Reality Transformed: Film as Meaning and Technique

Meaning in Life:
The Creation of Value
The Pursuit of Love
The Harmony of Nature and Spirit

The Nature of Love:
Plato to Luther
Courtly and Romantic
The Modern World

Mozart & Beethoven: The Concept of Love in Their Operas

The Goals of Human Sexuality

Santayana's Aesthetics

Essays in Literary Criticism by George Santayana (editor)

The Nature and Pursuit of Love: The Philosophy of Irving Singer
(ed. David Goicoechea)

IRVING SINGER

Mozart & Beethoven

THE CONCEPT OF LOVE
IN THEIR OPERAS

THE MIT PRESS
Cambridge, Massachusetts
London, England

© 2010 Irving Singer

MIT Press books may be purchased at special quantity discounts for
business or sales promotional use. For information, please email
special_sales@mitpress.mit.edu or write to Special Sales Department,
The MIT Press, 55 Hayward Street, Cambridge, MA 02142.

This book was set in New Baskerville by Newgen. Printed and bound
in the United States of America.

Library of Congress Cataloging-in-Publication Data

Singer, Irving.
Mozart and Beethoven : the concept of love in their operas / Irving
Singer.
    p. cm.—(The Irving Singer library)
Originally published: Baltimore : Johns Hopkins University Press,
c1977.
Includes bibliographical references and index.
ISBN 978-0-262-51364-7 (pbk. : alk. paper) 1. Mozart, Wolfgang
Amadeus, 1756–1791. Operas. 2. Beethoven, Ludwig van, 1770–
1827. Fidelio (1814) 3. Love in opera. 4. Music—Philosophy and
aesthetics. 5. Opera. I. Title.
ML3858.S49 2010
782.1092'2—dc22

                                                        2009014659

10 9 8 7 6 5 4 3 2 1

To Annetchu

Contents

CONTENTS

Preface to the
Irving Singer
Library Edition

In writing *Mozart & Beethoven: The Concept of Love in Their Operas*, I wished to unite three interests of mine: first, continued investigation into the nature of love and sexuality; second, explication of the relevance of such studies to the understanding of art works that express attitudes and affective inclinations pervasive in human nature, though not uniformly; and third, exploration of questions in aesthetics about the role of expression and meaningfulness in art, particularly as applied to musical drama of the operatic form. The first two overlap with the work I was doing in those years in relation to my trilogy *The Nature of Love*, which was completed ten years later, and also my book *The Goals of Human Sexuality*, which had appeared a few years before.

The latter had importance in the structural design of *Mozart & Beethoven*. The earlier text grew out of articles published in two scientific journals that specialize in sexological and biosocial research. Together with scientific material of that sort, *The Goals* introduced philosophical analyses and distinctions that were geared to issues in empirical sexology. The most prominent distinction was one I made between "the sensuous and the passionate," as I called them. I thought of these as two separate and very different aspects of sexual response. The sensuous issues from sensory faculties—most obviously, touch, sight, hearing, and the sense of smell—through which sexual desire shows itself and is partly constituted. In this modality, sex gives pleasure that can become very intense but usually remains cool, delightful, and more or less tame and sociable. The passionate is ardent and demanding, often impetuous, forceful, and imperious. Both are equally components of sexuality, and however much they contrast with each other, they are also compatible and capable of being harmonized in felicitous behavior.

In *Mozart & Beethoven* I experimented with the possibility of extending these ideas about the sensuous and the passionate to the human search for love as it is portrayed in the art of opera. In my later book *The Pursuit of Love,* I clarified much further the way in which the distinction might help us understand both love and sexuality, and more recently in *Explorations in Love and Sex* I enriched it with related analyses of compassion as an offshoot of love.

In this book I merely employ the distinction between the sensuous and the passionate as a convenient tool, a minimal device for ordering my perceptions and insights about musical and literary details of the operas I discussed. In the attempt, I studied both love and sexuality as functional components within the operatic art form. The resultant reflections could thus serve to demonstrate how even purely musical ideas interweave with the dramatic and literary effects that belong to this kind of art. Those in turn embody the human quest for meaning about the world and about oneself, which great artists like Mozart or Beethoven are able to transform into the creative works that audiences have appreciated as profound and truthful revelations of our nature.

The book sought to develop a new mode of understanding and experiencing the operas of Mozart and Beethoven by focusing upon their mythic and expressive elements. Though the distinction between sensuous and passionate might contribute to a useful perspective, I have always emphasized that it was only one among other possible implements, and that, in this case, mine was a *supplement* to what good literary and musical criticism regularly provides. Considering opera as an art that concentrates upon human feelings, the book analyzes the many ways in which music, language, and dramatic situation make a whole that conveys the character of emotional reality. For this effort, conceptual analysis is required, together with probing into the history of ideas and deliberation about affective phenomenology. Musicologists, music critics, and scholars in literature rarely have the training to do such work.

At the time that I was engaged in this venture, such writing was deemed very unprofessional by formalistic analysts. One reviewer of the book, a well-established professor of music, complained that I neglected the purely musical meaning in the masterpieces I studied. He maintained that he himself does not poach on the domain of reputable philosophers, and that he saw no justification for my poaching on his. Another professor told me that my methodology would encourage students to wallow in whatever emotionalism the music might evoke in them as they vaguely listened to it. As time went by, some experts in the field did recognize that there was a need for the kind of investigation that I made. In subsequent years their type of encouragement helped me to undertake the comparable writing that turned into my books on the art of film.

It seems to me egregious, in a mixed medium like the opera, to ignore the ways in which dramatic music functions within a larger context defined by the affective matrix of life itself. Formalists who treat their own expertise as the sole criterion of how one should and must write about operas would have to relegate to an intellectual limbo (or worse) the essays of Shaw, Stendhal, Rousseau, Schiller, Schopenhauer, Kierkegaard, Hegel, Nietzsche, Mann, Rolland, Turner, Sullivan, Rank (to say nothing of the vast preponderance of reflections by Berlioz, Wagner, and many other nineteenth- and twentieth-century composers)—in general, everyone whose point of departure is philosophical or speculative rather than technical and formalistic.

In the first sentence of the first chapter in *Mozart & Beethoven,* I announce the overall parameters of everything that will follow: "Though this book is not a study of libretti, it deals with concepts in the history of ideas, and therefore its approach to opera is more literary than musical." This immediately leads into a description of the perennial controversy about the relation between words and music in opera. After mentioning the opposing views of Mozart and Gluck, I use Wagner's remarks about an "inner blending" as an entry into my conception of metaphoric employment of both words and music in opera. Wagner was promoting his own type of music drama, and his terminology alone suggests the Romantic glorification of transcendental merging between disparate elements that recurs in all his creative work.

Trying to move beyond that perspective, I examine the expressive power that the joining of words and music attains when it relies on musical and literary metaphors that augment each other's mythological import. Moreover, as vehicles of expression, the sonic effects of music in opera differ from the use of words in poetry or dramatic speech. The former greatly magnify whatever affective meaning that is being communicated in some particular narrative. Opera fulfills this potentiality by deploying formal devices that recast and sometimes distort ordinary or poetic language for the sake of expressing feelings and emotions that are transmitted by means of these devices.

As an addendum to those ideas, the first chapter argues for the suitability of studying the erotic as it permeates the history of opera. At this point the distinction between sensuous and passionate enters as a possible source of enlightenment about opera's harmonization of words and music. The philosophical dichotomy provides a framework for elucidating not only the concept of love in the operas of Mozart and Beethoven but also the different mentalities of the two great men. Since those were present in their personal lives as well as in their musical productions, the chapter notes the playfulness in some of Mozart's letters and early compositions that salaciously mock the passionate, in contrast to the fervent missive to "the immortal beloved" that Beethoven wrote and never sent. The alternate orientations resurface in various ways throughout the operas of Mozart and in Beethoven's *Fidelio*.

Discussing the specific themes and motifs expressed in these operas, the remaining chapters avoid any neatly rigid delineations of their meaningfulness. Though I see in Mozart an extensive preoccupation with the sensuous, I also recognize his awareness and inspired portrayal of the passionate in crucial moments of his operas. And despite Beethoven's unfulfilled longing for the absolute oneness that fits the pattern of what nineteenth-century thinkers called love that is truly "Romantic," his musical imagination is also attuned to his own presentation of the sensuous.

The chapters on operas by Mozart make up almost half of the entire book. I do not cover all his operas, but rather concentrate on only the four most famous ones he wrote at the end of his life, plus *The Abduction from the Seraglio*. The first of these chapters is devoted exclusively to *Don Giovanni*, which it inspects as a high point in the myth of Don Juan. The legend more or less originates with Tirso de Molina's play *El Burlador de Sevilla* (*The Trickster of Seville*), which underwent many variations in the hundred and fifty years that preceded the libretto Mozart received from Lorenzo da Ponte. The myth itself is deeply embedded in human nature as it has evolved throughout millennia of the past and into the present. I focus upon the affective dimensions of this mythological continuity and its resonance in the details of Mozart's composition.

In relation to both the musical offering and the narrative, I discuss the implications of Don Giovanni's masculinity as well as its ability to enthrall those who respond to this individual as Mozart depicts him. Being a fictional personage who manifests both the sensuous and the passionate, he is an idealized icon of a male who feels no passion in his lovemaking but nevertheless captivates his female victims by professing passion for them and extending the promise of endless sensuous goodness they would accrue through sexual intimacy with him. I analyze Don Giovanni as someone who is passionate about the sensuous and who has learned how to use his know-how to attain the dominance over the other sex that many men crave. Don Giovanni is mythical in being a godlike image of a superman who loves no one, not even himself, but who pursues the art of seduction with a passionate delight in the sensuous pleasures that it affords him. As in the aria "Viva la Libertà," he proffers to all the women he has chosen as his playmates the freedom to experience this kind of sensuousness, which he enacts relentlessly and with religious dedication.

When his servant Leporello castigates Don Giovanni for deceiving women and causing them mental anguish once he deserts them, he says it's all love: "è tutto amore." I take him as speaking sincerely, and not with the arrogance that his words might imply. Christianity had taught that God is love and that his love is the explanatory principle imbued through nature as the ideal motive within human intimacy. As a mythological deity, Don Giovanni sees his conduct as definitive of love in action. Loving all women in his sensuous fashion, he indiscriminately bestows upon them the ability to have a passion for sensuous adventures that are commensurate with his. Having a conventional and second-rate mind, Leporello cannot undertand this. But Don Giovanni, belonging to a superior realm of erotic consummation, feels secure in his behavior.

When the Commendatore he has killed at the beginning of the first act gives him a chance to repent and mend his evildoings, he heroically refuses. He is willing to die as a libertine martyr rather than confess to any immorality, since that would be a betrayal of his heartfelt devotion. Mozart articulates the dramatic meaning of this magnificently. After regaling us with the sensuousness of Don Giovanni's music in all the previous scenes, and even at the beginning of the one in which the final confrontation occurs, Mozart ends the second act with the loud and horrifying sounds that express the Christian fear of hellfire and damnation. Thereafter, demons drag this Don Juan screaming to his fate in perdition, and Mozart tendentiously fills the epilogue with music that even Leporello would comprehend. It is music befitting the rejection on

moral grounds of either illegitimate passion or indulgence in the
bodily pleasures of the sensuous.

In the second Mozart chapter, I discuss the final masterpieces
he wrote based on two other libretti of Lorenzo da Ponte, and then
The Magic Flute supplied by Emanuel Schikaneder. My pages on
Don Giovanni had concluded with the suggestion that this operatic
black comedy combines *through the music* the antagonistic vectors
of the sensuous and the passionate. The last line in that chapter
reads: "What cannot be effected through mere rationality, or even
lived emotion, is thus accomplished through art alone." This then
becomes the guiding principle in my analyses of the affective dimensions in *The Marriage of Figaro* and *Così fan tutte*. At the same
time, I recognize that, splendid as all three of the da Ponte operas
are, their handling of the conflict between sensuous and passionate falls short of yielding a satisfying resolution.

Figaro, in Mozart as it was in Beaumarchais, mainly dwells
upon political struggles within the sensuous. The passionate does
get voiced by the vicious domination of the ruling male, the Count,
and by Figaro's irrational jealousy that vents itself in his diatribe
against women as a whole. But the pervasive scheming of Figaro
and Susanna monopolizes most of the action in the opera, and
at the end the sensuous wins out in the happy yet unimpassioned
marital culmination. Though the phenomenological structure of
Così is not the same, it is fundamentally similar. Despite the fact
that, in its portrait of the battle between the sexes, the possessive-
ness and fierce jealousy of the males have a more extensive role,
everything exists as part of their sporting competition with cynical
Don Alfonso abetted by the servant Despina, who do not believe
in passionate love. While the lovers are finally joined in marriage,
but possibly not to the persons they originally adored, the sensuous
philosophy of the two naysayers emerges clearly triumphant.

Beethoven did not approve of Mozart's da Ponte operas. He
said they were frivolous and even immoral. *The Magic Flute* he much
admired. He rightly saw it as a mythological completion of Mozart's
religious strivings. For Mozart the main religion of his final years

was the humanism in freemasonry. I interpret *The Magic Flute* as an intentional solution of the conflict between the sensuous and the passionate. Emulating both the music and the ideology of Mozart's opera, Beethoven constructed *Fidelio* as a paean to the brotherhood of man and the passionate love in a woman who is willing to sacrifice herself for the husband she is trying to save.

I call the Beethoven chapter "The Passion in *Fidelio*" in order to highlight its reverberations with the Passion of Christ. The personage who has suffered most is Florestan, whose torture results from his total dedication as one who fights for freedom from autocracy and the cruelty of the state. In the finale Leonora is hailed as a savior of mankind as well as the man she loves. In this regard, *Fidelio* is a mystic rite. It is a tribute to the passionate attitude that comprises the religious ingredient of what in my love trilogy I call "benign romanticism" as it developed in the first half of the nineteenth century.

That view about love could not be the ultimate resolution of affective problems in the modern world, but it sufficed to make Beethoven's singspiel the greatest of all operas about married love.

I. S.
April 2009

Preface

Though neither Mozart nor Beethoven was especially literary in his genius, both were alive to the intellectual stirrings of
their times. Mozart worked closely with his different librettists,
and Beethoven rejected text after text before he found the only
one he would ever use for an opera. In contributing to the ideas
and emotional attitudes of their libretti, Mozart and Beethoven
became more than mere transmitters of other people's thought.
They introduced their own vision of the world, and one cannot
fully grasp their achievement as creative beings without analyzing
the concepts they employed. That is what this book attempts to
do. Drawing upon various themes in the history of ideas, it exam-
ines moral, aesthetic, and erotic concepts that enter into some of
the major operas of Mozart and the one opera of Beethoven. It
tries to show how the concepts permeate the mentality of these
artists as well as the responses of their audiences.

The enterprise awakens several procedural questions. Can an
opera be seen from an extra-musical point of view without loss to
its aesthetic identity? Can Mozart and Beethoven be approached

through concepts that they themselves may not have recognized as part of their music? Should we separate the creations of the composer from the words of the librettist? And can anyone elucidate musical effects—even in a mixed medium like the opera—in terms other than those of precise musical analysis? In the first chapter, I briefly discuss these questions while attempting to describe the expressiveness of opera. Here I need only remark that since operas communicate through a *combination* of music, literature, and drama, they enact the conditions of life at a fictional level that cannot be reduced to any single discipline. They often lend themselves to a myth analysis that defies neat classification. If they are great works of art, they elicit pervasive responses that indicate their vast philosophical scope.

In seeking to understand the nature of these responses, the philosopher formulates problems that go beyond the work of art itself. These are problems about the human world in which all art originates and to which it returns by strengthening an audience's sense of reality. The philosopher's contribution is thus a supplement to musical and literary analyses, and it may have particular utility for understanding operas such as Mozart's and Beethoven's. Their audiences sought a type of aesthetic experience that is not provided by either concerts or ordinary dramas. The expressive character of opera results from a very special use of musical and literary elements, each of them serving the affective goals of a theatrical production. To appreciate opera's total impact, one requires a systematic approach to emotional and erotic realities that philosophy has often recognized as part of its domain. At this point, aesthetics merges with conceptual analysis and the history of ideas. The present book focusses upon the crossroads at which these three approaches converge.

An ideal spectator at the opera would combine the talents of a literary and music critic with the insight that comes from responding to human beings as they express their intimate feelings through a dramatic fusion of words and music. One sometimes doubts that this ideal spectator does or can exist. Sensitive listening for musical or literary meaning can undermine emotional response; and in an art that makes such massive assaults upon our feelings, the music or literary analyst may easily find himself distracted from that clarity of perception which he naturally prefers. This alone may reveal what is most interesting about the opera: *by its very nature, it would seem to make impossible demands upon all conceivable audiences,* to say nothing of the performers.

In their various activities all theorists and critics work at this difficulty. My essay does so by studying concepts of love that are particularly relevant to the operas of Mozart and Beethoven, and therefore to our appropriate experience of them. And though the problems, both human and aesthetic, of Mozart and Beethoven were not identical with those of other composers, we may find that a similar method can recommend itself for the understanding of Wagner, Verdi, Berlioz, Stravinsky, etc. The realization of this possibility reaches beyond the scope of this little book, however, and the same must be said about the more complete analysis of the concept of expression which these pages do not themselves attempt. Careful readers will notice that I tend to use the terms *expression* and *expressiveness* as if they were synonymous. In subsequent work, I hope to pursue the implications of their diversity of meaning. The concept of love in Mozart and Beethoven is not affected by this further analysis, but important issues in aesthetics depend upon it.

Compared to these possible developments, the current study has a relatively modest goal. It will have succeeded if it can reveal something of the conceptual framework that structures Beethoven's one opera as well as the most frequently performed operas of Mozart. It may be read either as a phenomenological exploration into human affect or as an interpretive essay about several great works of art. In trying not to duplicate the methods of literary or music criticism, it offers a different kind of approach that may nevertheless be useful as a companion to these disciplines.

In delineating the perspective from which I write, my first chapter suggests that opera attains its excellence by supplementing the expressive inadequacies of language by means of music while also supplementing the conceptual inadequacies of music by means of language, both elements being controlled by the necessities of the drama. If this is true, one needs a consecutive way of understanding the affective realities that underlie these dramatic necessities. My distinction between "the sensuous" and "the passionate" provides me with a convenient tool for that investigation. In the Mozart operas I find a prolonged conflict between sensuous and passionate aspects of the erotic life; and in Beethoven's *Fidelio* I see a new attitude towards passion, one that leads into the romanticism of the nineteenth century while also trying to resolve the problems that preoccupied Mozart and others in the eighteenth century. To show how opera in those two centuries expresses human feelings, one can use different distinctions and different types of conceptual analysis. I offer mine as one among many that may be viable, and in the hope of encouraging others to develop alternate perspectives more meaningful to themselves. Here, as elsewhere, my approach is wholly pluralistic.

I have been extremely fortunate in the friends and professional associates who have helped me—directly or indirectly—in this work. Apart from the expert assistance of my wife, I have benefited from comments, criticisms, and diverse modes of encouragement that were graciously provided by John Harbison, Fred Lerdahl, Richard A. Macksey, Isaiah Berlin, Leonard Bernstein, David Epstein, Ruth Cigman, A. R. Gurney, Peter Kivy, Frederick Morgan, Paula Deitz, W. J. Bate, and Harold J. Hanham. An earlier version of part of the first chapter was read before an annual meeting of the American Society for Aesthetics. I have also profited from participation in two MIT Faculty Seminars at which parts of the book were discussed: one was called The Cambridge Humanities Seminar, directed by Eugene Goodheart and Alvin Kibel; the other was the Faculty Seminar on Music, Linguistics, and Aesthetics. I am grateful to the administrators, professors, and students who contributed to these life-enhancing experiments in mutual education.

I. S.

Mozart & Beethoven

THE CONCEPT OF LOVE
IN THEIR OPERAS

CHAPTER I

Opera & Expression

1. *Dramma per Musica*

Though this book is not a study of libretti, it deals with concepts in the history of ideas, and therefore its approach to opera is more literary than musical. This immediately raises questions about the nature of operatic art. Nowadays most people assume it is the music and not the words that principally determine an opera's aesthetic value. One writer even asserts that "when words enter into music they are no longer prose or poetry, they are elements of the music."[1] Mozart probably thought the same. In one of the letters to his father, he emphatically states that "in an opera the poetry must be altogether the obedient daughter of the music."[2] But if one holds this position, one can only be baffled by attitudes that prevailed at other times. For instance, in his preface to *Alceste* Gluck advocated quite a different relationship between words and music. As Gluck puts it, "I sought to restrict music to its true function, namely to serve the poetry by means of the expression—and the

---

[1]Susanne K. Langer, *Feeling and Form* (New York: Charles Scribner's Sons, 1953), p. 150.
[2]*The Letters of Mozart and His Family,* trans. and ed. Emily Anderson (New York: Macmillan, 1966), II, 773.

situations which make up the plot—without interrupting the action or diminishing its interest by useless or superfluous ornament."[3]

These two attitudes are usually thought to be contradictory. They would seem to voice incompatible generalizations about the very nature of opera, its aesthetic structure and inherent being as an art form. And certainly these statements of Gluck and Mozart are relevant to different *kinds* of operas. But possibly opera in general can encompass both varieties. For clearly Mozart is not advocating "useless and superfluous ornament" in the music; and it is significant that Gluck wants music to serve poetry "by means of the expression." Gluck is trying to eliminate musical elements that diminish an opera's dramatic power. Mozart is trying to exclude literary effects that cannot be articulated in music and therefore subvert its expressiveness.

One could thus argue that the question of priority is not as important as either Gluck or Mozart may have thought. In all essentials the two may really agree. Composers often talk about their art as if there were no way of practicing it other than the one that they themselves pursue. For each of them, creating from his own perspective, this may well be true. What serves as convincing autobiography, however, need not be taken as universal aesthetics.

Similar considerations apply to the contradictions that would seem to separate Wagner from Stravinsky. Wishing to synthesize the thesis of Gluck with the antithesis of Mozart, Wagner formulated a notion of music drama in which poetry and musical expression would undergo an "inner blending." Though Wagner seems to have vacillated about the relative importance to be given words or music, he constantly envisaged the writing of operas which would match these elements as ingredients that merge with one another. One might immediately remark that Gluck and Mozart also sought a perfect blending between words and music. But it was Wagner that Stravinsky and other neoclassicists reacted against in writing works that sought to *separate* words and music, treating them as elements that were to retain their independence instead of melting together. In choosing Latin for *Oedipus Rex*, Stravinsky reports that he no longer felt "dominated by the phrase, the literal meaning of the words." He claims to have emancipated himself from the words as anything but "purely phonetic material." Far

[3]Reprinted in *The Essence of Opera*, ed. Ulrich Weisstein (New York: W. W. Norton, 1969), p. 106. Previously, Monteverdi had also said: "Let the text be the master of the music, not its servant." See Reinhard G. Pauly, *Music and the Theater* (Englewood Cliffs: Prentice-Hall, 1970), p. 55.

4

from thinking of the text as an alter ego with which his music should merge organically, the composer could now "dissect it at will and concentrate all his attention on its primary constituent element—that is to say, on the syllable."[4]

Wagner advocated his approach as a way of revealing an underlying unity of feeling which characterized reality, and Stravinsky defends his method as an austere style that prevents music from falling into sentimentalism. Properly understood, each of them is right in what he says and what he does. For their doing is the creation of works of art, and their saying is part of the self-assertion that gives one the courage to create one's own type of art. Taken as aesthetics, however, their statements are often inaccurate. For instance, one could very well argue that Stravinsky separates words and music only to recombine them for new expressive purposes. When he makes Queen Jocasta's proud speech sound hootchy-kootchy at times rather than purely regal, he attains his own kind of merging between words and music. The effect may not be sentimental, and it may even seem cynical when compared with Wagner's romanticism, but it too depends upon musical expression. It is more than just the abstract use of phonetic material.

Once we see how misleading these contrary theories have been, we may discover ways in which their insights can be harmonized. The earliest term for opera was *dramma per musica,* and it is the word *per* that may provide the basis for agreement. For all the different theories of opera recognize the importance of presenting drama *through* the music, by means of it, and therefore by virtue of musical expressiveness. It is in this capacity of music to express both ideas and feelings that we shall find the distinctive characteristics of opera, in Mozart and Beethoven as well as other great composers.

2. Metaphor

I will not be saying much about nondramatic music. Abstract music, like abstract painting, expresses fragmentary and indeterminate feelings. The intricate designs to which these feelings contribute are quite different from what one finds in works of art that explicitly depict human events. In the opera, music is "applied," in the sense that it has a function within a dramatic totality. Each

[4]Igor Stravinsky, *An Autobiography* (New York: W. W. Norton, 1962), p. 128.

mood, feeling, emotion expressed in the music pertains—either directly or indirectly—to the enactment of human situations. One might also say that the abstract in music becomes vital or lived, inasmuch as its expressiveness is now used to communicate the flow and fluctuation of some presented experience. While organizing sounds as formal patterns, music in the opera uses them to portray and to magnify the affective universe through which human beings confront one another.

In this regard, consider the famous letter in which Mozart writes about his music for *The Abduction from the Seraglio*. After mentioning that he has composed the music for Osmin with a certain performer in mind, one whose voice was renowned for its excellence in the lower bass range, Mozart describes how he makes Osmin's rage into something comical. He says that this effect will be achieved by giving Osmin's first-act aria an accompaniment of Turkish music—in other words, by creating an incongruity between the enraged intensity of the vocal line and the tinkling playfulness in the orchestra. But also, Osmin's rage is expressed in a way that divests him of his dignity and causes him to appear ridiculous. In showing how the music does this, Mozart writes to his father:

> The passage "Drum beim Barte des Propheten" is indeed in the same tempo, but with quick notes; but as Osmin's rage gradually increases, there comes (just when the aria seems to be at an end) the allegro assai, which is in a totally different measure and in a different key; this is bound to be very effective. For just as a man in such a towering rage oversteps all the bounds of order, moderation, and propriety and completely forgets himself, so must the music too forget itself. But as passions, whether violent or not, must never be expressed in such a way as to excite disgust, and as music, even in the most terrible situations, must never offend the ear, but must please the hearer, or, in other words, must never cease to be *music*, I have gone from F (the key in which the aria is written), not into a remote key, but into a related one, not, however, into its nearest relative D minor, but into the more remote A minor.[5]

Mozart is here describing some of the means by which expressive music portrays human emotion and therefore human reality. The relationship between the music and what it depicts is not especially mimetic, for there is only a limited attempt to copy actual

---

[5]*The Letters of Mozart and His Family*, II, 769.

sounds. Osmin's voice goes up and down just as it would if he were an angry man in the real world, and his quick notes duplicate the agitated sound of an authentic rage; but the expressiveness of Mozart's music consists in more than imitation alone. It results primarily from the use of auditory signs that function in a metaphoric rather than a literal manner. There is nothing in actual anger which corresponds *directly* to a change in key. Yet in changing keys, Mozart is doing something to the music which suggests a parallel change in the condition of the man. Like an enraged person, the music would seem to "forget itself" inasmuch as it violates certain harmonic and tonal conventions. This is not at all the same as having a tantrum. Going from the key of F into one that is more or less remote is only figuratively similar to an improper or immoderate manifestation of aggressive emotions. The former expresses the latter, however, because both deviate from norms of expectation.

Though these norms are not the same, one dealing with music and the other with manners, they are alike in deriving from recognized conventions that serve as a basis for generalization; and once we intuit this metaphoric link, we have no difficulty in perceiving the operatic effect. Through the drama we see Osmin being angry, and through the mimetic properties of the music—the loudness, the rapidity, the stamping sounds—we know that it too is portraying his anger. From the relationships between tempi, rhythms, key changes, etc., we then infer those nuances of character that Osmin's anger expresses.

It is because the expressiveness of music goes beyond its mimetic capacity that Mozart can freely choose between related and remote keys. His decision determines the nature of his metaphors; it is more than just a means of protecting tonal sensibilities in the audience. Later composers have been more daring about the making of unpleasant noises. But whether it shocks or soothes the listener, an opera's ability to express human feelings will always depend on the metaphors it formulates rather than on attempts to duplicate sounds.

Berlioz makes a similar point in his essay "The Limits of Music." In discussing musical imitation of physical reality, he lays down four conditions for its proper employment: first, that imitation of this sort shall never be an end but only a means—never the main musical idea but only a complement to it; second, that imitation should be limited only to phenomena particularly worthy of attention; third, that imitation should be precise enough to avoid

7

misconception; and fourth, that "physical imitation shall never occur in the very spot where *emotional* imitation (expressiveness) is called for, and thus encroach with descriptive futilities when the drama is proceeding apace and passion alone deserves a voice."[6]

Berlioz illustrates this last limitation by citing a momentary lapse in Beethoven's *Fidelio*. While Leonore and Rocco are digging the grave in Act II, they encounter a large rock and have to roll it aside. In a figure for the double basses of the orchestra, Beethoven imitates the dull sound of the stone being rolled. Berlioz calls this imitation "a sad piece of childishness." His judgment may be too severe, but of greater importance is the reason he gives for making it. He says that imitation is here an end in itself; it contributes "no poetry, no drama, no truth." In short, it is mere copying and therefore lacks the expressive power that might have been achieved through imaginative use of musical metaphors.

3. Words, Music, and Magnification

In his letter about Osmin and the way in which his rage has been expressed, Mozart remarks that the music was composed before any words had been written. He makes it very clear that he was not setting music to words but rather getting Stephanie (the librettist) to write the words that he needed for this aria. Mozart says this in the same mood in which he speaks of poetry as the obedient daughter of the music. But as far as expressiveness is concerned, it does not matter what gets written first, nor even whether the composer has written the words himself. For obviously Mozart had in mind—from the very outset—some dramatic characterization which was to be conveyed by the right words in relation to the right music. Even Gluck would not have suggested that a composer submit to just *any* words that are presented by his librettist. They must always be words that will further the ultimate aim of expression. Where they come from, or when, is immaterial.

Similarly, it would be a mistake to think that the expressiveness of operatic music can be appreciated without the words. To listen to an opera for the music alone is like listening to a foreign language that one does not know, hoping to understand what is being

[6]Reprinted in *Pleasures of Music*, ed. Jacques Barzun (New York: Viking, 1951), p. 245.

said by watching the accompanying gestures and body movements. Certainly these are an important part of the communication, and one can also admit that music in an opera is *more* important than mere gestures in a spoken language; but the fact remains that opera is a type of dramatic performance which cannot be fully appreciated unless one understands its verbal impact.

In saying this, one need not deny that great poetry is usually detrimental to great opera. Various theorists have pointed out that vocal music requires a concentration upon musical sounds which is defeated by the mental processes that must be directed towards the best poetry. W. H. Auden even speaks of the ideal libretto as a "private letter" that the librettist addresses to the composer rather than to the public.[7] In part, at least, Auden means that the words must not seek to be interesting in themselves, as they would if they aspired to poetic excellence, but only as a vehicle for musical enjoyment.

In my opinion, Auden's formulation is confused. Though the words in an opera do have importance only as they enable the audience to perceive what is being expressed by music, they are far from being a private communication to the composer. They must be understood, and even savored, by the audience if it is to appreciate how the composer uses them for the sake of musical expression. Of course, one could *refuse* to take an interest in the words, as if one were listening to a concert. But then one would not be having the experience of an opera. Aesthetically there would be something wrong, as there is with all works of art if one fails to respond to the complexities of their particular medium.

How, then, are words related to music in an opera? It is sometimes said that the music in an opera stands to the words in a similar relationship as poetry to prose. There is a measure of truth in this. One need only imagine a prose version of Shakespearian lines on the one hand, and an operatic version on the other, to detect how music resembles poetry in adding expressiveness to ordinary language. Try the experiment with the following:

> Full fathom five thy father lies;
> Of his bones are coral made;
> Those are pearls that were his eyes;

[7] W. H. Auden, "Notes on Music and Opera," in *The Dyer's Hand, and Other Essays* (New York: Random House, 1962), p. 473.

9

Nothing of him that doth fade
But doth suffer a sea-change
Into something rich and strange.
[*The Tempest*, I, ii]

There are many prose versions that might communicate a comparable meaning as effectively as Shakespeare's lines. They would be inferior, however, in their ability to express that welter of elusive feelings which the poetry exquisitely conveys. By means of alliteration, rhyme, meter, and other formal devices, the lines suggest a regularity of structure in nature itself, an orderliness that may even govern disasters such as drowning. One feels that this cosmic order may arise from intelligence and possibly prescience, as in the making of poetry itself, and therefore that this occurrence of death is meaningful and not absurd. There is even the suggestion of a beautiful outcome to the event, eyes turning into priceless jewels by some agency of artlike creativity. At the same time, a sense of mystery, a feeling of wonderment, lingers in these lines. What to us is hideous in nature takes on an uncanny loveliness once it is subsumed under aesthetic imagination. Poetry is able to achieve this special expressiveness partly because it prevents us from speaking the lines (or hearing them in our inward ear) with the flatness of insignificant discourse. The lines must be intoned, voiced as tonal vehicles, enunciated for that play of vowels and consonants which adds a musical dimension to what would otherwise be meaningful but only prosaic.

Without limiting ourselves to actual vocal or operatic versions of Shakespeare's lines, we can easily imagine how different songs would express a variety of feelings relevant to them. One might accentuate the loveliness, another the mystery, still another the sense of prearranged orderliness, and so on. As in poetry, the vocal music goes beyond prose in its capacity to express feelings vividly. But musical versions differ from the poetic in having a larger range of tonal effects which tend to *magnify* the element of expressiveness. It is as if each of the affective components in the poetry—the emotions, the feelings, the rudimentary sensations—were enlarged for the sake of emphasis and immediate recognition. This, I think, is the reason why great poetry does not lend itself to the making of great libretti. Either the poetry would be distorted by the process of magnification, or else the music would have to strain for conceptual effects that are too precise, too minute for it to express. Even the delicate characterizations achieved by the music in Mozart's operas are not as detailed or extensive as they would be in poetry alone.[8]

This disparity between poetic and musical expression also accounts for opera's special affinity to the stage. We often feel that reading Shakespeare in private can yield an aesthetic experience which a staged performance may possibly fail to provide. For the poetry can be read at home as well as heard in the theatre, and often with greater understanding. Poetic effects can always distract one from what is happening on stage, and what is happening offstage can always deflect one's attention from the intricacies of poetry. With the opera, all this is quite different. What happens may be more remote from ordinary life than in verse drama, since people rarely sing themselves through emotional situations, and therefore operatic presentations always run a greater risk of appearing ridiculous. But even so, an opera must be seen as well as heard. Unlike a verse play, it *has* to be performed; and a practiced musician who reads the score will generally keep that in mind. Even when we listen to a recording or a broadcast on the radio, we project ourselves into an imagined performance. The magnification in operatic expressiveness partly results from this theatrical context which opera always presupposes. If only because it is louder, it covers the stage and pervades the theatre in a way that verse drama cannot. This is the opportunity of opera; and in art, a relevant opportunity is always a justification.

4. The Performing of Emotions

T. S. Eliot thought that poetic and musical expression both differ from prose in their ability to take us "beyond the namable, classifiable emotions and motives of our conscious life when directed towards action."[9] To say this, however, is to suggest that feelings belong to at least two categories: one pertaining to the world of action, and the other being a fringe that we become aware of, as Eliot says, in a "temporary detachment from action." Doubtless some such distinction can be made, for there are innumerable ways in which feelings may be analyzed, and no matter how we define "action" and "detachment from action" they will surely involve different kinds of feeling. Nevertheless, no distinction of this

[8]On opera as magnification, see Leonard Bernstein, "What Makes Opera Grand?" in *The Joy of Music* (New York: Simon & Schuster, 1959), pp. 266–303.
[9]*Poetry and Drama* (Cambridge: Harvard University Press, 1951), p. 42.

sort can do the work that Eliot intended. Poetry and music are alike in vividly articulating feelings or emotions that prose might fail to emphasize; but the feelings and emotions themselves are not necessarily of a different kind. On the contrary, prose turns into poetry once the feelings in our ordinary life are given a linguistic expression that does articulate them vividly. And when music carries the process further, it merely provides a different means of presentation. The feelings and the emotions need not be those that belong to a psychic fringe or peculiar state of detachment. They are the same affective responses that occur throughout our active life— feelings precisely of the sort that a biologist or psychologist would find characteristic of man's existence in his environment. They are not themselves special; they are merely treated in a special way and elicited within the special situations of poetic or musical expressiveness.

Opera is often maligned as an "impure" art, and of course, it is a *mixed* art. But its purity—that is, its excellence as an art form— consists in its ability to supplement the expressive inadequacies of language by means of music while also supplementing the conceptual inadequacies of music by means of language, both elements being controlled by the necessities of the drama. This does not mean that opera is aesthetically better than either unaccompanied music or unaccompanied language. It only means that it does something different. D. F. Tovey argues that even the expression of emotions can be more powerful in abstract music than in the opera, where one has to put up with the machinery of the stage and all those theatrical makeshifts needed to get characters into position for the singing of an aria. But the examples that Tovey gives—a moment in a Brahms quartet or a Beethoven sonata—are instances where music expresses emotions in a way that is simply foreign to the opera.[10]

What, then, is the value of Tovey's comparison? Disputing that one form of music is more powerful, has more "emotional force," than the other seems to me less rewarding than recognizing that each is a *different* way of expressing emotions. I suspect that artistic success depends upon the composer's genius within his chosen medium rather than an absolute ranking among the media themselves. And in fact when Tovey talks about Mozart's achievement in his operas, he never suggests that the imperfections of musical

---

[10]Donald Francis Tovey, *The Main Stream of Music, and Other Essays* (New York: Oxford University Press, 1949), p. 173.

drama prevented Mozart from writing great expressive music there as elsewhere.

As opposed to critics like Tovey, some writers have thought that only in dramatic works can emotions be adequately expressed by music. One can see why they may have taken this extreme position. In symphonic or chamber music expressive elements are present but not clearly related to emotions as we encounter them in ordinary life. In an oratorio the music generally expresses feelings for the sake of underlining a message or making a ritual statement. In a single song, or even a song cycle, the music expresses individual moods, possibly a succession of them, but we do not see emotions acted out, portrayed before us by actors in a scene. The performing of emotions is more readily available to the dramatic imagination, and consequently to the opera as a dramatic phenomenon. What the composer loses in having to make do with the exigencies of the theatre, he regains by having human beings in lifelike circumstances as instruments that supplement the ones in the orchestra. In life we all have within us, as Hamlet says, "that which passeth show"—emotions that we cannot express fully and that conventional society hardly recognizes. In the opera, however, dramatic personages shriek their anger and scream their joy. They do so in sounds that are not only expressive but also socially acceptable. For now these utterances belong to the domain of art as well as life.

5. Myth and Erotic Phenomenology

Operas are to the modern world what Greek tragedies, which also contained musical elements, were to the ancient. In none of the other arts do the feelings of men and women exhibit themselves with the same mixture of publicity and privacy. For though the opera exposes affective impulses that everyday life obscures, it also hides their detailed idiosyncrasies through the sheer abstractness of musical sound. I think this is the kernel of truth in that line from Schopenhauer which is often quoted. Music, he says, "does not express a particular and definite joy, sorrow, anguish, delight, or peace of mind, but joy, sorrow, anguish, delight, peace of mind *themselves,* in the abstract, in their essential nature, without accessories, and therefore without their customary motives."[11] By expressing emotions that are specific in the drama but only generic in

[11]*The World as Will and Representation,* I, no. 52.

the music, the opera enables its audience as well as the characters to undergo a series of inchoate and ambiguous catharses that need never reveal their actual origins.

In *Don Giovanni* there is a moment in which Mozart and Da Ponte seem to affirm something to this effect. In Act I, scene iii, Don Giovanni, Donna Elvira, Don Ottavio, and Donna Anna attest to the expressive nature of music when they jointly sing of "a feeling of unknown anguish" that intimates a hundred things of which it cannot speak. Elvira mentions "anger, fury, spite, fear," but we know that even these general terms are too specific. The anguished feelings pertain to what is happening in the plot, of course; but also the characters are commenting upon their sheer capacity to express emotions *per musica*. While explicating their feelings, they are also referring to the condition of every personage in an opera. As a recent critic states: "For eighteen bars (9.31–49) they all pay tribute to the power of music to mean what words cannot say."[12]

Mixing privacy and publicity in this way, operas approximate mythic performances. They often rely upon myths for their libretti, and in much of the seventeenth century they were required to draw their subject matter from mythology. In a myth the overt story is a mechanism for articulating a view of reality which the audience shares with the performers and the author. The emotions expressed are both specific and general. Intellectual rigor, realistic representation, detailed description of the social order—all this is subordinated or even falsified for the sake of engulfing us in the emotional matrix which gives a myth its permanence throughout human variability. In an opera much of this mythic content is conveyed through the literary concepts out of which the story is constructed. Responding to the myth in his own way, the composer provides a tonal reformulation of these concepts. At the same time, his music also leads us to suspend our disbelief, our sense of separateness. It washes over everything that induces skepticism about the myth. Where the emotive impact is so strong and the auditory sensations so beguiling, how can we in the audience withhold assent?

In all myths the affective elements are generally the most important, and opera accentuates them through the process of expressive magnification. In some operas, such as *Tristan and Isolde*, the original narrative disappears to an extraordinary degree, as a means of allowing these affective elements to dominate completely.

[12]Robert Moberly, *Three Mozart Operas* (New York: Dodd, Mead, 1968), p. 187.

Writers like de Rougemont are mistaken when they claim that all music since Mozart is sexual, but one could very well argue that almost all opera has been erotic (in a fairly broad sense of that word) since its origins in the Florentine Camerata. Not only were the texts drawn from love literature, but also the music became progressively more suggestive and even sexually arousing. Some works in the nineteenth and twentieth centuries may reflect a reaction or contrary influence; but from the time of Monteverdi to the present, operas have regularly devoted themselves to dramatizing myths of love prevalent in the western world.

In view of the importance which these mythic and erotic elements have had in the opera, it is remarkable that so little has been done to understand them. Musical analysis has often been used to show how the composer contributes to the dramatic totality; and the libretto, as a literary artefact similar to the script of a play or the scenario of a film, is finally beginning to receive serious attention.[13] One now needs a systematic way of seeing how music, words, and dramatic situation can make a unity that conveys affective mythologies. For this purpose it scarcely matters whether one thinks of the creative artist as the composer, since he usually has the final word in the production, or as a team consisting of composer and librettist. Mozart working with Da Ponte is no longer Mozart writing sonatas on his own. As one can study Mozart as a dramatist,[14] so too must one recognize that Da Ponte influenced the music Mozart composed. Their collaboration succeeded because they experienced and could portray an integrated world of human feeling. Their works express a mythic vision common to them both, basic to the music as well as the libretto, and immediately accessible to the audiences for whom they wrote.

This mythic vision cannot be wholly codified, for it exists in the diverse attitudes towards life which define a continuing culture. In dealing with the concept of love, Mozart and Da Ponte drew upon a long tradition that told them which feelings or emotions were to be expressed. The tradition was available to them at the same level of imagination that governs all myths. We can study the process with some assurance because the mythologies of western culture have been written down in works of literature and philosophy. As we

[13]See Patrick J. Smith, *The Tenth Muse: A Historical Study of the Opera Libretto* (New York: A. A. Knopf, 1970).

[14]On this, see Joseph Kerman, *Opera as Drama* (New York: Vintage Books, 1956).

shall see throughout this book, one cannot fully understand the operas of Mozart and Beethoven apart from this development in western civilization.

There is, however, no single way in which mythic concepts must be approached. Their domain is extremely vast, and different theorists will investigate them on the basis of individual predilections. Approaching the opera in terms of the erotic imagination, I shall be using a distinction that I developed in an earlier book.[15] I there described two kinds of attitudes that often overlap but are clearly separable from each other. One I called "the sensuous," the other "the passionate." They influence the way we experience the world, and they contribute to symbolic expression in all areas related to human affect. They are especially relevant to works of art such as the opera.

By the sensuous, I refer to the surface phenomena of sensory gratification. Through it people enjoy one another without emotional involvement, or any other involvement beyond the pleasurable use of one's sensory equipment. All erotic possibilities are made accessible by means of our senses; and though the effort may be futile, we sometimes try to limit our enjoyment of another person to the delights that mere sensation can provide. For that matter, we may even wish to eliminate other people from our sensory enjoyment. But whether or not it tends towards solipsism, the sensuous is a way of approaching erotic and affective experience *as if* it were nothing but sensation.

By the passionate I refer to the strong and ardent feelings that are generated by our need for oneness with another person. In ways that cannot be explained by surface sensation alone, human beings crave and yearn for each other, strive and struggle to possess one another. We long to participate in the being of other people. At various times we experience powerful and demanding desires which manifest our need for affective oneness. This complex of emotionality has always been recognized as the source of all human passions.

Both the sensuous and the passionate show themselves in the overt mechanisms of sexual behavior. They therefore lend themselves to physiological as well as psychological analysis. But since they are pervasive aspects of human nature, they also appear in works of art that are not explicitly sexual. The sensuous and the

[15]*The Goals of Human Sexuality* (New York: W. W. Norton, 1973; London: Wildwood House, 1973; paperback ed., New York: Schocken Books, 1974).

passionate take on special importance in media—such as the opera—that devote themselves to the expression of feelings. A staged performance can show us the drama of affective response like no other art (except for the cinema). In being both abstract and expressive, however, music enables the drama to avoid the pruriency that comes from presenting sexuality too concretely. An opera can thus involve the audience in extremely intimate feelings without requiring it to consider sexological details. At the same time, we watch and listen as persons whose nature cannot be rigidly dematerialized. We experience the opera as erotic creatures, though it would be absurd to think that what happens in the theatre can be reduced to what happens in the bedroom.

There is a school of aesthetics which maintains that art is just the sublimation of forces that control us in the real world. Freud spoke in these terms because he accepted an hydraulic model of psychological energy and because he assumed that biological goals were more fundamental than any others. If one dispenses with these articles of faith, however, one may consider all experience—and in particular, the aesthetic experience of opera—as affording unique and equally valid access to human reality. The mythic structure of many operas can be analyzed as a presentation of sensuous and passionate phenomenology; but this must not be taken to mean that these operas merely sublimate a physiological drive to satisfy the sensuous and the passionate, or even that the sensuous and the passionate manifest themselves more clearly in sexual behavior than in the symbolic effects a dramatist or composer may use as elements of his art. Human nature is too complex, too fluid, and too dynamic to warrant any such reductivism.

It is also the case that human nature changes through time. And therefore one could possibly argue, as some of my own critics have, that the distinction between the sensuous and the passionate is itself a product of the last two centuries. I use it as a handy tool for the sake of expressing what seems to me real and important in the world as I know it. If the distinction has utility for understanding Mozart or Beethoven, this *may* be due to developments (intellectual as well as emotional) which began in the late eighteenth century and which I share with these two great men as fellow denizens of the modern world. But I doubt that the distinction must be limited to a single period of history. In any event, we need not linger on this problem. For present purposes it will suffice if we can attain a new and suggestive approach to the genius of Mozart and Beethoven, employing whatever implements we may find.

17

Throughout the investigation, the reader must always remember that feelings in an opera express themselves through the
musical and dramatic structure. At no point should he detect a conflict between what I shall be saying and what a musical analyst
might wish to offer. One can reveal the erotic expressiveness of the
duet *Là ci darem la mano* by analyzing Mozart's use of chromaticism
and slurred notes to indicate Zerlina's uncertainty, a sturdy melody
in A major to express Don Giovanni's seductive assertiveness,
dark-sounding horns to warn the girl that he may be tricking her,
fluent woodwinds to help the Don ingratiate himself, the two voices
approaching until they almost overlap, eventually uniting as she
succumbs to his promise of love, etc.[16] The merits of such analysis
are obvious and undeniable. But it always presupposes that we
know about real as well as fictional seducers, the assertiveness expected of males in the eighteenth century, the alleged uncertainty
of females, and in general those concepts of love which pervade the
Don Juan legend that Mozart's opera inherited from Tirso de
Molina, Molière, and many others. Music and libretto making a
dramatic totality in *Don Giovanni,* the affective elements that consti-
tute its basic mythology belong to each of them—or rather, to both
in their interrelationship. In elucidating this aspect of an opera, the
method I employ is different from, but totally congruent with, the
musical and literary approaches it seeks to supplement.

6. Mozart and Beethoven

Incomplete as they are, these ideas about *dramma per musica*
may serve as a framework for investigating love in the operas of
Mozart and Beethoven. I turn now to the men themselves. Works
of art are not reducible to the artists' personality, but some of the
relevant differences between Mozart and Beethoven as composers
can be seen in letters that reveal their erotic dispositions. Consider
first Mozart's correspondence with his wife Constanze after years

[16]For useful analyses of this sort, see Charles Hamm, *Opera* (Boston: Allyn &
Bacon, 1966); J. Merrill Knapp, *The Magic of Opera* (New York: Harper & Row,
1972); and Boris Goldovsky, *Bringing Opera to Life* (New York: Appleton-Century-
Crofts, 1968), particularly pp. 65–105 ("The Language of Music"). See also the
chapters "Serious Opera" and "Comic Opera" in Charles Rosen, *The Classical Style:
Haydn, Mozart, Beethoven* (New York: W. W. Norton, 1972). Rosen argues that in the
Mozart operas "music as [an equivalent for the] dramatic action takes precedence
over music as expression" (p. 289), but he does not deny that Mozart consistently
used his operatic music to express feelings relevant to the drama.

of marriage. For instance, a letter dated May 23, 1789, runs as follows:

> On June 1st I intend to sleep in Prague, and on the 4th—the 4th—with my darling little wife. Arrange your dear sweet nest very daintily, for my little fellow deserves it indeed, he has really behaved himself very well and is only longing to possess your sweetest. . . .* Just picture to yourself that rascal; as I write he crawls on to the table and looks at me questioningly. I, however, box his ears properly—but the rogue is simply . . .* and now the knave burns only more fiercely and can hardly be restrained. Surely you will drive out to the first post-stage to meet me?[17]

This playfulness about the body belongs to the sensuous mode. So does the suggestion that a part of the body has a life of its own. If the "little fellow" burns fiercely for Constanze's sweet nest, it must be he and not Mozart who feels passion. Mozart himself pretends to disdain what the "knave" impetuously desires; he is even prepared to box his ears. We know that Mozart is only joking and that he plays at castigating his own body in order to affirm his love for the body of Constanze. But also his mode of expression is designed to titillate the erotic imagination of his wife, and his own, in a way that protects them both from the actual ferocity of the ardent passion he claims to feel. Thriving on the cooler feelings of playfulness, the sensuous is more pleasant and agreeable than the passionate. It turns the longing of a painful separation into a comic (and therefore manageable) need to house the male organ of sexuality within the female.

This attitude towards marital sex reappears in the little vocal quartet *Caro Mio Druck und Schluck,* which Mozart also wrote in 1789. To music that is plaintive and mock-serious, Mozart creates a farcical scene in which he and his wife take leave of one another while mixing German and Italian, sense and nonsense, expressions of a sorrowful parting and references to how they will defecate in desperation:

CONSTANZE:
Caro mio Druck und Schluck,
Caro mio Schluck und Druck,
Ti lascio, oh Dio! kugelrund,
Che affano! a Loth ist ka Pfund.

---

[17]*The Letters of Mozart and His Family,* II, 928-29. *Editor's Note: "Each dotted passage represents a word which has been blotted out in the autograph."

Quello l'adira,
Wir können nix dafüra,
Cara Cobotchi,
Pietà, es ist schon achti,
Un pò di carità,
Sonst machen ma . . . ! a, a, a

[Darling Squeeze-and-slurp,
Darling Slurp-and-squeeze,
I leave you, O God! You tub,
What torment! Half-an-ounce is not a pound.

It's infuriating,
We can't do anything about it,
Dear Cobotchi,
Heavens, it's eight already,
Have a little mercy on us,
Or else we'll shi-i-! Ah! Ah! Ah!]

MOZART:
Cara mia bagatellerl,
Io parto, tu resti, Spitzignas,
Oh Dio! tu resti, Spitzignas,
Che pena! che tormento!
Wenn's regnet, ist's nass.

[Darling tinkle-toy,
I leave, you stay, Pointy-nose,
O God! You stay, Pointy-nose,
What pain! What sorrow!
When it rains, it's wet.]
[Mozart then repeats Constanze's last six lines above.]

As I will show hereafter, Mozart often subjects the passionate to this kind of ridicule. As it here speaks in a hybrid gibberish, so too does it frequently appear as madness in the operas. How different all this is from the letters to the "immortal beloved" that were found in a drawer of Beethoven's desk after his death. Written in 1812, when Beethoven was 42, these letters were never mailed, and scholars have disagreed about the identity of the addressee. For our purposes, the following lines may be treated as if they were written to no one in particular, and as an outburst of passionate longing that would never spend itself with any woman:

My angel, my all, my very self! . . . Why this deep sorrow, where necessity speaks? Can our love subsist otherwise than by sacrifices, by our not desiring everything? Can you do anything to alter the fact that you are not wholly mine, that I am not wholly yours? Oh, God! gaze at the beauties of Nature and reconcile yourself to that which must be! Love demands everything and quite rightly so; that is how I feel towards you and you towards me. Only you so readily forget that I must live for me and for you. . . . [Following day.] My thoughts surge towards you, my immortal beloved, now joyfully, then again sorrowfully, waiting to know whether fate will hear us. I must live with you entirely, or not at all. Yes, indeed, I am resolved to stray in distant places until that moment when I can throw myself into your arms and say that I am really at home with you, when I can send my soul, wrapped in your presence, into the realm of the spirits. Yes, unfortunately there is no other way. You will not give in, for you know my fidelity to you. Never shall another be able to possess my heart, never—never! Oh, God, why is one forced to part from her whom one loves so well![18]

This evident contrast between Mozart and Beethoven has been discussed by Romain Rolland, who argues that "Mozart had every kind of feeling, but he had no passion—except his terrible pride and a strong consciousness of his genius."[19] Rolland quotes a letter in which Mozart says that "composing is my one joy and passion"; but it is mainly in the music itself that Rolland purports to find the lack of strong emotions towards other human beings: "There is nothing extravagant or romantic about Mozart's love; he merely expresses the sweetness or the sadness of affection. As Mozart himself did not suffer from passion, so his heroes are not troubled with broken hearts. The sadness of Anna, or even the jealousy of Elektra in *Idomeneo,* bear no resemblance to the spirit let loose by Beethoven and Wagner. The only passions that Mozart knew well were anger and pride. The greatest of all passions—'the entire Venus'—never appeared to him." Later on, Rolland adds: "There is, however, some sensuality in Mozart. Though less passionate than Gluck or Beethoven, he is more voluptuous."[20]

Even if Rolland is right in separating Mozart and Beethoven along the lines of the sensuous and the passionate, it seems bizarre for him to say that the *only* passions Mozart knew well were anger

[18]*Beethoven: Letters, Journals and Conversations,* trans. and ed. Michael Hamburger (New York: Anchor Books, 1960), pp. 102, 104.
[19]Romain Rolland, *Essays on Music,* ed. David Ewen (New York: Dover, 1959), p. 245.
[20]Ibid., p. 255.

and pride. Rolland himself quotes from that letter of Mozart's in which he describes the love music he had just written for *The Abduction*. As the letter clearly shows, Mozart felt that in Belmonte's aria he had caught the spirit of sexual passion; and in the music, as in his description, he treats it with respect. Throughout Mozart's operas, the passionate often asserts itself. As against Rolland's generalization about Mozart's erotic phenomenology, one should consider the contrary opinion of Stendhal. In his "Letter Concerning Mozart," written in 1814, Stendhal emphasizes the deep feeling that pervades the later Mozart operas. He comments upon the "urgent and heart-felt passions" of the characters in *Figaro;* and according to Stendhal, these passions far exceed anything Mozart received from Beaumarchais's original. In *Don Giovanni,* which he considers a work of "Mozart's wholly romantic imagination," Stendhal particularly relishes the element of terror. He suggests that the libretto for *Così fan tutte* would have been perfect for Cimarosa but "it was totally unsuited to the genius of Mozart, for whom love was never a laughing matter. Love, for him, was at all times the passion that could make or mar his life. His interpretation revealed only one side of the characters, their tenderness of heart."[21]

Quite obviously, Stendhal is responding to something in Mozart which Rolland did not find equally important. Rather than trying to adjudicate between them, however, I wish to see *how* the sensuous and the passionate enter into Mozart's operas. They function differently in different works, and their conflict with one another creates aesthetic as well as psychological problems. By analyzing the structure of these problems, one can also chart the development in Mozart's outlook on the world. At the level of affective mythology, his operas may be seen as the expression of human attitudes that go beyond music and engage the erotic as well as the artistic imagination.

In Beethoven one encounters a vision of reality quite different from Mozart's. Not only are there temperamental differences between these two men, but also Beethoven belongs to an era that was evolving a new system of values. Beethoven repeatedly remarked that Mozart's Da Ponte operas were immoral and unworthy. But *The Magic Flute* he revered as a great achievement of the human

[21]Stendhal, *Haydn, Mozart, and Metastasio,* trans. Richard N. Coe (New York: Grossman, 1972), p. 206.

spirit. He rightly saw it as the culmination of Mozart's thought, and he took it as a basis for developing his own ideas in *Fidelio*.

How, then, do the sensuous and the passionate enter into these operas? *Don Giovanni* presents their conflict in the most striking manner. For Beethoven no less than Mozart, it is an appropriate starting point.

CHAPTER II

Mozart: The Conflict in *Don Giovanni*

1. A Passion for the Sensuous

In studying the Don Juan myth, Kierkegaard discusses the nature of sensuousness in ways that are highly suggestive. He treats it as "an immediate stage of the erotic," something that precedes and often precludes marriage, a moment in the dialectic by which mankind eventually propels itself towards the love of God. Kierkegaard identifies the figure of Don Juan, and in particular Mozart's *Don Giovanni*, as *mere* sensuousness, isolated from the later stages of the erotic, authentic for what it is but troublesome in its arrested condition.

Kierkegaard's concept of the sensuous is not exactly the same as the one I employ, but his ideas are worth pursuing. He thinks that Don Giovanni's mythic embodiment of sensuousness becomes possible only when spirituality excludes the sensuous while also recognizing the function it performs at its own level. He expresses this notion as follows: "When sensuousness appears as that which must be excluded, as that which the spirit can have nothing to do with, yet without passing judgment upon it or condemning it, then

24

the sensuous assumes the form of the daemonic in aesthetic indifference."[1]

In saying this, Kierkegaard refers to the idea (which he had previously stated) that Christianity brought sensuousness into the world as that which the spirit rejects and indeed *defines* itself by rejecting. Prior to this rejection, the sensuous had no distinction of its own. It was merely a part of the pagan search for harmony with nature, as in Greek mythology. "In the Greek consciousness, the sensuous was under control in the beautiful personality, or, more rightly stated, it was not controlled; for it was not an enemy to be subjugated, not a dangerous rebel who should be held in check; it was liberated unto life and joy in the beautiful personality."[2] With Christianity all this changes. The sensuous becomes an erotic *something,* that which is excluded by the spirit, and a character like Don Juan becomes possible as its dramatic enactment. Because the spirit defines itself by rejecting the sensuous, it does not condemn the sensuous. It needs it as the figure needs the ground, as the positive needs the negative. It therefore allows the sensuous to express its own daemonic being and permits a detached observer to enjoy the spectacle in an amoral, areligious way—i.e., in "aesthetic indifference."

Taking this attitude, Kierkegaard does not attack or vilify Don Juan. His English translators alert the reader to the fact that he employs the term "sensuous" rather than "sensual" as a way of avoiding all moral issues: "His Don Juan is not guilty of sensuality but simply represents sensuousness—an amoral wild impulse following its purely natural urge ... an obscure, elemental force of nature."[3] At the same time, however, Kierkegaard nowhere suggests that man may suitably remain at this elemental stage. Despite the systematic ambiguity of his either/or, we always feel that dialectical momentum which seeks to propel us toward religious transcendence. Kierkegaard approaches Don Juan much as the Catholic tradition approaches Heloïse and Abelard and, indeed, all sinners who are saved by the magnitude of their sin no less than the glory of their redemption. The greater the one, the more magnificent the other. Sooner or later, we are expected to draw the conclusion: If human beings can bestow such importance upon one

[1] Sören Kierkegaard, *Either/Or,* trans. David F. Swenson and Lillian Marvin Swenson, rev. by Howard A. Johnson (New York: Anchor Books, 1959), I, 89.
[2] Ibid., p. 60.
[3] Swenson and Swenson, eds., p. 447.

another, what must it be like to love God and to be loved by him in return?

But there is something wrong with this approach. For the sinners—whether Don Juan or Heloïse and Abelard—do not think in these terms, and neither does the communal ideology that arrogates to itself the dignity of representing man's spirituality. Society condemns Don Juan, passes judgment within the drama as well as without. Mozart's opera, which Kierkegaard considers to be the only genuine version of the myth, is significantly entitled *Il Dissoluto Punito*. What could be more explicit?

Furthermore, Kierkegaard's notion that the sensuous principle comes into being only after Christianity seems somewhat dubious. The literary legend of Don Juan dates from the seventeenth century, possibly from the late Renaissance, but the *myth* extends into the backward abyss of time. It expresses problems that have existed as long as there have been men and women; it belongs to the pagan world as much as the one we live in. As if he were the Statue committing Don Juan to hell, Augustus exiled Ovid and banned the *Ars Amatoria*. In similar fashion, the Socrates of Plato's *Symposium* castigates the wildly promiscuous Alcibiades, Athens' military and erotic hero who went into battle with a portrait of Eros emblazoned on his shield. Many other examples could also be given. Kierkegaard is mistaken to assume that only with Christianity does the sensuous become "an enemy to be subjugated." But he is right to associate the *legend* Mozart and Da Ponte used with problems that exist primarily within the Christian dispensation. Ovid was banished for having encouraged adultery, not for treating lovemaking as a sensuous art. Alcibiades is condemned for squandering his *passion* on one human being after another. Promiscuity itself is not a problem for Socrates or Plato. On the contrary, they see it as a means of detaching oneself from particulars and thereby achieving a universal love of goodness in all things.

In Christianity, however, sexual morality makes new demands: first, the avoidance of both adultery and promiscuity; and second, the elimination of all passion—except in the love of God. In effect, this reduces ideal sexuality to sensuousness within the bonds of matrimony. In portraying Don Juan as a sinner, the legend (clearly established by Tirso de Molina's play *El Burlador de Sevilla*) attacks him for violating the orthodox attitude towards sex. His sinfulness consists not only in promiscuous or adulterous behavior, but also and more specifically in the fact that he pursues the sensuous with the kind of passion that was authorized only for the love of

26

God. Spirituality having forbidden earthly passions though con-
doning pleasures of the senses, Don Juan offers the *reductio ad
absurdum* of sensuousness becoming a dedication no less passionate
than the spiritual itself. He is daemonic as a parody of the Christian
vocation, a mocking suggestion of a life that men and women might
actually prefer. As Kierkegaard called the true believer a Knight of
Faith, so too is Don Juan the Knight of Sensuousness. He has a
passion for the sensuous just as the saint had a passion for holiness.
He feels no passion for any of the women he seduces, just as the
saint can feel no passion for human beings in general. If Christianity dispatches Don Juan to the fires of damnation, it is because
he represents the greatest of all possible temptations: he does the
right thing for the wrong reason, exterminating passion towards
other persons but then refusing to direct it towards the Christian
God. Instead, he turns the passionate back upon his own appetites
and makes the sensuous into the object of a new spirituality.

To say this much, however, is to say that Kierkegaard neglected the humanistic import of both the legend and the myth.
Like other idealists in the nineteenth century, he could only see the
sensuous as a stage on the way to religious passion. He could not
imagine its becoming a religion in itself. Yet this is what Don Juan
confronts us with; and in *Don Giovanni* his glittering heresy becomes manifest through the immediacy of great music. Kierkegaard considered Mozart's opera an achievement that "takes the
highest place among all classical works." Would he have said that if
he had realized how truly subversive it is?

2. The Sensuous as a Part of Male Dominance

In moving beyond Kierkegaard, we must first reject his belief
that Mozart and Da Ponte represent the Don Juan myth with
greater authority than Tirso or Molière.[4] Nor does the temporality
of music make it more suitable—as Kierkegaard thought—for presenting this as opposed to all the other myths of love. Finally, Kierkegaard is mistaken in limiting Mozart's opera to a single principle.
The mythology of *Don Giovanni* is not restricted to the sensuous

[4]See my essays "Molière's Dom Juan," *The Hudson Review*, Autumn 1971, and
"The Shadow of Dom Juan in Molière," *MLN*, December 1970. See also Micheline
Sauvage, *Le Cas Don Juan* (Paris: Éditions du Seuil, 1953), and Georges Gendarme
de Bévotte, *La Légende de Don Juan*, 2 vols. (Paris: Hachette, 1906–29).

alone, or even to sensuousness in its dialectical conflict with the passionate. Though basic to the opera, the drama of this struggle is always an overlay that molds another system of human problems. For one thing, notice that the protagonist is a man—just as Phaedra, in that myth about the perils of passion, is a woman. Why should this be? Are women any less sensuous than men? For hundreds of years poets, philosophers, theologians, and many others had been condemning women for their wily ways in sex, their sinful sensuality. In Mozart's opera, however, there is no female equivalent of Don Giovanni. Though Zerlina feels the lure of the sensuous, neither she nor any of the other women defines herself in terms of it. Don Giovanni does; and since he holds the opera together, it is always *male* sensuousness that provides the dramatic focus of the work.

Even so, Don Giovanni represents more than just the sensuous male. If he were nothing else, his myth would have remained at the level of the picaresque novels. Mozart's opera goes beyond them in treating sensuousness not only as a passion but also as a passionate expression of male dominance. In the traditions that characterize the western world, masculine aggression towards the female has often been ontological as well as social and sexual. Men (not all, but many) have assumed that *by the very nature of their being* they are superior to women, and tacitly at least, most women have agreed. Men have allowed themselves a freedom of thought and behavior that only they could enjoy, and with few exceptions, women in the past have thought they were right to do so. If male dominance—by which I mean the fact that men have insisted upon an inherent superiority and that women have acquiesced in this unverifiable belief—belongs to the world we have inherited, the effects of this ideology have nevertheless troubled men and women at all times in history. By the eighteenth century, women were beginning to raise their voices, either opposing male freedom or else demanding something similar for themselves. And some men were also dissatisfied with the traditional dogma: it did not assure them of any lasting supremacy, and it occasioned guilt feelings they could not control.

Don Giovanni bristles throughout with the tension and the nervous energy of this dilemma. But even at the end, nothing has been resolved. Though Don Giovanni is eliminated, the institution of male dominance continues unabated. For Don Giovanni dies not at the hands of women—as in the Orpheus myth—but through a metaphysical agency that represents *another kind* of masculine domination. The Statue destroys Don Giovanni as a way of denying that supremacy can be attained through mere sexuality. The Commendatore, Ottavio, and even Masetto dominate by means of a *social* authority that Don Giovanni constantly rejects. For them it is political strength that provides the foundation of their dominance over women: they are the warriors, they run the state, they assert their prerogatives as fathers and husbands. For Don Giovanni such evidences of orthodox power are valuable only as instrumentalities. Given the necessity, he will fight with the Commendatore and even kill him. But such achievements, which others might take as a final indication of manliness, do not afford the kind of dominance that matters to him.[5]

What then does Don Giovanni really want? In the context of the opera, it is very clear that he wishes to assert his potency as a male by *playing* with women. He plays with them for the same reason that a cat plays with a mouse: in order to demonstrate that he is in control. And since the playfulness of love shows forth the sensuous, his passion continues as long as he is able to keep on playing. Critics have often pointed out that in the opera itself Don Giovanni never manages to seduce anyone. Others claim that offstage escapades with Zerlina, Elvira's maid, Leporello's girlfriend, and even Donna Anna should be counted to his credit. But all this is immaterial. What matters is the fact that throughout the work Don Giovanni continues to play the game. He is a professional athlete with a very high batting average, and every moment that he is on stage—whether he is succeeding or failing in some particular effort—we *see* him as such. He is a hero simply by virtue of his reputation as an erotic sportsman. That he encounters frustrations within the opera simply shows how difficult the sport is.

To deal with love, or at least lovemaking, as if it were just a game is not uncommon among men. Despite the technology of contraception, it is difficult for a woman to separate coitus from its biological base. Though she may ignore the facts of reproduction and be as sensuous as anyone could wish, she cannot prevent sexual behavior from penetrating her entire body. For a man the situation is different, if only because his sexual physiology is more highly localized. He may therefore use his sexuality as a means of scatter-

[5]On this, see *G*, a novel by John Berger (New York: Viking, 1972). For an interpretation of the Don Juan legend as "an assertion of male power and strength against women who are both desired and feared," see David G. Winter, *The Power Motive* (New York: The Free Press, 1973), p. 175 and passim.

ing potency abroad, sowing fertile fields that he can always leave behind, invading, conquering, and then withdrawing for reasons of his own.

Male sexuality *need* not be a game or a sport. It can be a commitment, a culminating oneness, a creative act more worthy than any other. But I daresay that most men have not recognized it as such. Though in fact they may be Masettos and Commendatores, they easily identify with Don Giovanni and think of their sexuality as a game. For that enables them to impose their own rules upon the activity. Games are not permanent. They come to an end and may be renewed with someone else. This in turn allows men to emancipate themselves from female control, each encounter with a woman being used as a means of escaping a previous one. Considering sex as just a game also means that no failure can be terribly important. One may succeed the next time, or the next.

Don Giovanni expresses this masculine concept by treating love as something inconsequential, a passing event that proves one's virility but little else. In his *dramma giocoso* ("playful melodrama"), Mozart presents us with the most serious of human conditions and then treats it in the most jocular way possible. What to Donna Anna, Elvira, and even Zerlina is shattering, frightful, unbearably tragic—all this is to Don Giovanni merely fun and games. And the more frantic the woman becomes, as in Elvira's first aria, the more ridiculous she appears, not only to the men who overhear her but also in the music that Mozart gives to the orchestra. Elvira is simply not playing the game. Indeed she hardly seems to realize there *is* a game to be played. And neither do the other women in the opera.

What distinguishes Don Giovanni from ordinary men is the fact that he does nothing *but* play this game. He is also more imaginative at it than anyone else. Treating sex as something external to himself, he shows how one can always put it on and take it off. Don Giovanni does this by creating a series of masquerades. In the first scene, he wears the mask that enables him to play at being Don Ottavio, Donna Anna's suitor. She tries to unmask him, but he swears she will never learn who he is. As we know from *Cupid and Psyche, Lohengrin, Rumpelstiltskin,* and all those other fables in which the male seeks to keep his identity secret, the game of love requires anonymity. Even Leporello hides, saying that he must not be seen. For both him and his master, sex is always faceless, fleeting, nocturnal, and deceptive. One must pretend to be something one is not—a lover, a suitor, a spouse. The game consists in carrying out the performance without the commitment, in what Kant would call purposefulness without a purpose.

In the second scene, the sport changes slightly. It now consists in escaping the dissatisfied beloved. Women being snared by a delusion about their uniqueness, their ardor cools once they are treated as part of a collectivity. To free himself of Elvira, Don Giovanni has Leporello recite the *Aria del Catalogo*. It slackens her pursuit by showing her that she is only one among many. The trick works, and Don Giovanni eludes her temporarily.

In the next scene he plays a different kind of game. In this one, the player tries to seduce a girl while pretending to be the other, more conventional type of male. Don Giovanni poses as a kindly aristocrat who arranges the festivities of marriage between Zerlina and Masetto. The trick is to carry this out in such a way that one eventually displaces the bridegroom and gets the girl oneself. The manoeuvre fails when Elvira returns and gives the game away.

Far from being deterred by such difficulties, the Don brings the whole neighborhood into his sport. He gives a party to which everyone is invited. His opponents appear, themselves masked as if to counter Don Giovanni's deceptiveness. He ignores them and continues his play for Zerlina. The game now consists in outwitting the jealous husband, Masetto, by making love to his bride under his very eyes. Special talent is needed for this, and both Leporello and his master remark: "Here one needs to use one's brains." As one of his devices, Don Giovanni plays at being a peasant. With Zerlina he performs a country dance, lowering himself to her social level, whereas earlier he had offered to raise her to his own. When he fondles Zerlina in the dark and she screams for help, he pretends that the culprit was really Leporello—once again playing at being the aristocrat who is above such things.

In the next act, this playful substitution between master and servant becomes central to the opera, and much of the remaining plot employs the theme of double masquerading. The game has become more complex (though less intricate than in those earlier versions of the myth which had Elvira disguise herself as a man). Here, in the second act, Don Giovanni gets Leporello to woo Elvira in his disguise, and then he woos *her* servant in the disguise of Leporello. As with Zerlina, Don Giovanni is playing upon the sexual equality of different social classes: Elvira's maid is as much a female as her mistress. They are both subject to domination by the male, even a male like Leporello. But then Don Giovanni uses the masquerade as a means of asserting his superiority over other males as well. Disguised as Leporello, he beats up Masetto and tries to seduce Leporello's girlfriend. He even expresses an interest in Leporello's wife, a move that balances Leporello's sporting with Donna Elvira. When master and servant finally return to their own identities, in the graveyard, they play another game. In this one, statues are treated like living persons. But this game, whose rules Don Giovanni can hardly fathom, brings an end to his sporting life. It leads to death, where all masks are removed and the game of sexuality no longer makes sense.

It is in the nature of his existence that man cannot have quiescence or final success. Each fulfilment leads to a new appetite, and that requires further striving. To striving itself there is no end other than death. For me at least, these elementary facts explain Don Giovanni's sexual sport as well as anything else. Within the symbolism of the myth, what counts as ultimate victory is the seducing of the female. Not only does this elude Don Giovanni throughout the opera, but also the entire action arranges itself into a dialectic of his nearly succeeding, suddenly and dramatically failing, and then bounding off for a fresh attempt. Stendhal wisely perceived that in order to be a Don Juan one must take the same interest in winning women "as one does in winning a game of billiards."[6] But in Mozart's opera the billiard ball is Don Giovanni himself. His ability to profit from each angle, each cushion, and the curvature of every movement provides the unity within this work of art.

The entire opera is thus strung together by Don Giovanni's frustrations, and by the fact that these redirect his trajectory without terminating it. At the outset he is stopped by Donna Anna's resistance to his lovemaking; then he is checked by Donna Elvira's surprise appearance. At the end of each of these scenes, he runs off; and that becomes the pattern for the rest of the opera. He makes love to Zerlina, is thwarted by the intervention of Elvira, and the two women run off. Don Giovanni runs after Elvira when it looks as if she will disclose too much to Donna Anna and Don Ottavio. Later he returns to the siege of Zerlina, is stopped by Masetto, but deftly gets them both to skip into the ballroom. When his seduction fails again and he is confronted by the avengers, he ends the act by running out of the building. In the serenade scene, he terminates the love-play of Leporello with Elvira by making them run away.

[6]Stendhal, "Werther and Don Juan," in *On Love* (New York: Grosset & Dunlap, 1967), p. 256.

His own efforts with the maidservant having been interrupted by the peasants, he has them run off in various directions. After beating up Masetto, he runs off himself. In the courtyard scene, the unmasked Leporello runs away from his captors. And in the final scene, Elvira runs away from Don Giovanni while Leporello runs away from the Statue. Here, at last, Don Giovanni refuses to run. He stands his ground, as if he too were a statue. At that point, he dies, much as Faust does when he accepts the beauty of the passing moment and stops struggling for future possibilities.

Since Don Giovanni personifies the playfulness of male sexuality as it seeks to dominate the female, perhaps it is preferable that he seduces no one in the opera. Given the nature of the enterprise, none of his conquests would indicate very much. That is why he must endlessly seek to renew them, like Sisyphus pushing his stone uphill. This can be represented better by a series of failures than by successes. Stendhal says that Don Juan's life must eventually become boring. Possibly he is thinking of the character in Molière, or of that tedious catalogue. In what we see before us, however, there is no question of boredom in the mythic figure that Mozart and Da Ponte have created. The opera contrives to give him a stage existence that never lacks for movement and excitement. He and the music both are always on the go. His frustrations are exhilirating to him, not depressive or wearisome. Boredom is something that neither he nor the audience has time to experience. The game was constructed with precisely that in mind.

3. *Viva la Libertà*

But what, exactly, is the purpose of the game? I have described it as a male attempt to assert dominance over the female by means of sensuous sexuality. But this could occur in different ways: everything from physical violence and political enslavement to the subtlest kind of brainwashing. Don Giovanni's method is seduction. Like a peacock that flashes its bodily attire before the female of the moment, he glitters and glows throughout the opera. In the Champagne Aria his suavity seems especially dangerous, but even so he remains—as always—bright, witty, and wholly congruent to feminine sensibilities. If the game consists in *winning* the woman, it nevertheless involves her complicity. Don Giovanni not only wants to impose his will upon the female; he also wants her to accept and corroborate his type of sexuality. This can hardly be achieved by

33

threats, but it can be effected through sensuous allurement. Don Giovanni understands the phenomenon because he understands women. He is in tune with them, and even seems to like them indiscriminately. Though the psychoanalytic idea that Don Giovanni is "really" a homosexual cannot be supported by anything in the opera, his attunement to female sexuality does give rise to the homosexual joke about his "great secret": i.e., that he really is a *lesbian*. Why? Because he likes women. At one point, Leporello begs his master to leave them alone. To which Don Giovanni replies: "Leave women alone? madman! leave women alone? You know that they're more necessary to me than the bread I eat, more than the air I breathe!"

This kind of remark need not be limited to its pathological overtones. Certainly Don Giovanni is obsessed by women as some people are obsessed by television or the stock market. Certainly his ability to smell a woman's odor before he can see her—as in the first scene with Elvira—is not a normal acuity. But Don Giovanni also needs women as all men do. He has made this need into a profession, much as the troubadours or romantic poets of the nineteenth century did. Unlike them, however, he makes love to women for the sake of professing faith in *himself*, in his own sexuality as a male, rather than in any female object of his choice. He needs women to confirm and ratify his faith. Like all who proselytize in the name of a holy cause, he must have as many believers as his evangelical message can reach. He must therefore seduce every woman he meets, convert her to his sacred calling, prove its legitimacy by means of her submission. He needs women as Christ needs sinners—as the living evidence of his mission, and as the occasion for his distinct and peculiar bestowal.

For this reason, I think we must treat the conversation between Leporello and Don Giovanni quite seriously. Having heard that his master finds women more necessary than the air he breathes, Leporello says: "And you have the heart then to deceive them all?" Don Giovanni sensibly replies: "It's all love; whoever is faithful to one is cruel to the others; I, who feel such ample sentiment in myself, love all of them; and since women don't comprehend these things, they call my natural goodness [*buon natural*] deceit."[7] In the

---

[7]Wolfgang Amadeus Mozart, *Don Giovanni*, trans. Ellen H. Bleiler (New York: Dover, 1964), p. 151. In general, translations from the libretti are my own; but I found it so hard to improve upon Ms. Bleiler's translation that I used it whenever possible and convenient. Her edition also includes useful background information. See also Alfons Rosenberg, *Don Giovanni: Mozarts Oper und Don Juans Gestalt* (Munich: Prestel Verlag, 1968).

original, Don Giovanni says women "calcolar non sanno": they don't understand these things because they do not know how to count beyond the one that is themselves. Just so had Molière's Dom Juan claimed that what he believed in was two and two making four and two fours making eight. Sganarelle, the forerunner of Leporello, concludes that his master's religion is arithmetic. Even if this were true, however, the religion of Mozart's character is nothing like arithmetic. It is simply faith in that "natural goodness" of which he speaks, his infinite appetite, his ability to delight in *any* number of women. Leporello doubts his master's sincerity, and we too may wonder how much good he actually provides. Yet it would be a cardinal error to ignore this *buon natural* in terms of which Don Giovanni justifies his existence. It is the basis of his mythic power, too great a quantity for any single woman. It sustains everything in the music as well as in the text.

Who then is this man, and how does he represent other men? Until we can answer such questions, it will be hard to separate his natural goodness from deceit, or his passion for the sensuous from the crudest kind of self-adulation.

Let us begin with the fact that all men are born of woman. From birth are dependent upon a biological subspecies significantly different from their own. The long period of protection required by human beings in their youth makes it both necessary and difficult for the male to emancipate himself. For little girls the problem is not equivalent, since they have the same maturational pattern as their mothers and know from an early age that they will be women themselves one day. The young girl may not *want* to emulate her mother, but she always can. The boy's condition is more precarious. He cannot live without the aid of a dominant mother, he cannot fully identify with a father who excludes him from the world of adults, and yet he feels a need to explore the universe on his own, to venture beyond the family, to create a society that he can control by himself.

As a consequence of this condition, male sexuality is frequently motivated by an unresolved desire to attain freedom from sociobiological dependency in childhood. Wishing to free himself from women, the male may seek to dominate them; and since his sexuality is merely a tension within his body having no instinctive end that he clearly understands, he is always tempted to use it as a means of liberation rather than commitment. From this there arises the concept of *libertà*, which in *Don Giovanni* signifies the attaining of freedom through sensuous sexuality.

But freedom is an elusive concept. How can a man be sure that he has achieved it, assuming that it can be achieved at all? In different cultures, different evidences will be taken as definitive. In the western world, the male has often reassured himself by making two kinds of sexual demands: first, that women admire his erotic excellence, his sensuous charm and physiological potency; and second, that they succumb to it in the sense of being so passionately aroused that they lose self-control. From the first demand arises masculine exhibitionism, sexual boasting, quantitative interests in the number of seductions, the frequency of orgasms per night, the length of the penis, etc. Sexuality then appears as one among other types of achievement. It is something the male *does,* and therefore reveals his ability to survive as an active animal in the midst of physical nature. It provides proof of his capacity to capture prey. This also explains the second demand, that the woman change from a restrictive and moralizing mother-figure into an infinitely receptive concubine with worms in her vagina—as *The Arabian Nights* puts it—thereby reducing her to a helpless bundle at his feet. These demands are designed to provide a sense of freedom. Whether the man screws the woman, as if she were in need of carpentry, or plays her like a violin, as the adolescent boy hoped to do in *The Catcher in the Rye,* sex becomes a device for "possessing" the female and thereby liberating oneself from her domination.

In saying that men want freedom of this special sort, I do not doubt that they want other things as well. They want to feel that at least one woman will constantly trust and admire them. They want to know that she will always be available. They want to commit themselves to an erotic bond based upon mutual and enduring love. They want the pleasures of paternity, and they want a social role that will enable them to supplant their own fathers. In the Commendatore, Don Ottavio, Masetto, and even Leporello, these aspirations are quite apparent. Only in Don Giovanni are they completely absent; and that is why he ultimately affects us as a monster, a dazzling and a brilliant creature but a monster nonetheless. At the same time, he is the only one who represents the need for freedom. Only he recognizes its relevance to male sexuality; and only his sexuality has any importance in the opera. In being sensuous with every woman, Don Giovanni remains free of all women at once. And though we may desire the contrary as well, this is something that resonates in every man.

The idea of running symbolizes this need for freedom, but Don Giovanni's character also appears in the way in which he confronts his death, his *loss* of freedom. Each of the two acts ends with some such confrontation. In the finale of the first act, the avengers threaten Don Giovanni with his coming destruction; he senses its approach but defiantly insists upon an ability to clear all obstacles. And in fact, he marvelously escapes. At the end of the second act, he can escape no longer; but he refuses to repent and does not waver in his determination. He does not fear death because he sees in it just another adventure, a further means of running away. It is the final freedom: through it he escapes all the women who have been pursuing him, to say nothing of all those new ones he would have been constrained to seduce in the future.

Just before he dies, Don Giovanni drinks to the "glory of mankind," much as he had toasted "la libertà" in the first act. On both occasions he is drinking to the glorious virility in himself, the freedom and the natural goodness which death can overcome but only by destroying it. Discussing the earlier toast, de Rougemont is astounded by the fact that Donna Anna, Donna Elvira, Don Ottavio, and Leporello all join in even though the interests of the first three conflict with Don Giovanni's.[8] Why then do they raise their voices in that "Viva la libertà"? I think the answer lies in the fact that these are the principal characters of the opera, and so they must articulate its single most important concept. Mozart gives the ensemble vigorous and bright music without the slightest touch of doubt or indecision. The quest for male freedom is fundamental to the mythology of this opera, and they sing to it in the only harmony these diverse characters are able to achieve. They are not expressing *allegiance* to Don Giovanni, or to his way of achieving freedom. The avengers are still his sworn enemies. But they all recognize the potency of freedom itself. It sustains them in their being as characters in this particular work. It creates the dramatic world in which they live. Without it, they would have no parts to play. They would not exist. It is, in short, their reigning divinity; and whatever their personal motives, they worship it just as the ancients of both sexes worshipped the priapus.

This supervening freedom I have sought to interpret as a male phenomenon. But men have always accorded some women sexual freedom comparable to their own. Since it is important for a man to feel that women accept him in his own sexuality, he wants to believe that they do so freely—as if their own sexual needs were automatically satisfied in the process of gratifying his. Men hunger for, and

[8]Denis de Rougemont, *Love Declared: Essays on the Myths of Love,* trans. Richard Howard (Boston: Beacon, 1963), p. 156.

often demand, a sensuousness in women correlative to their own. They may even crave an aggressiveness on the woman's part that both emulates and justifies their own need to dominate. If the woman cannot respond, the male attitude easily turns into sadism. But whether or not this happens, the man's need for freedom may force him to liberate women in some respects while dominating them in others.

It is this, I think, that explains Don Giovanni's strange combination of cruelty and sympathy towards the female sex. Stendhal understood the condition very well. In a footnote to his study of the Don Juan personality, he says: "Cruelty is only a diseased form of sympathy. *Power* is only the greatest happiness, after love, because one imagines that one is in a position to *command sympathy*."[9] In relation to the suave Don Giovanni, this may at first seem paradoxical. For he is not cruel in the manner of a Scarpia or a Marquis de Sade. He does not torture his victims into submission, and he never threatens them with social or psychological reprisal. He merely seduces them, and this he does by being charming. He is nevertheless cruel towards all of his women—for he knows what his faithlessness will mean to them—and his cruelty comes from a diseased attempt to elicit love. He wishes to control one woman after another in order to attain an infinite power over their sympathy. He thinks he manifests such power by playing with them sensuously, and by leaving them once intimacy has been established. As a matter of fact, the women all desert him sooner or later, and his search for freedom brings only fugitive pleasures. He is a man who can never stop running.

4. The Daemonic in Don Giovanni

Various critics have argued that Don Giovanni must be seen as a force or abstract principle and not as a person. Compared to the protagonists of Tirso or Molière, Mozart's seductive male does seem remarkably undelineated. We learn a great deal about his search for sexual freedom, but very little about those individual characteristics that would enable us to identify him as a person. Kierkegaard believes that this is because Don Giovanni never rises above the category of "pure" sensuousness. According to Otto

[9]"Werther and Don Juan," p. 260.

Rank, he is a fertility god whose powers of fecundity have been so cheapened by the restraints of Christianity that he now appears as a mere scamp or libertine. Ortega and de Montherlant tend to think of him as a sexual abstraction: that which is wholly virile in men, something that responds to the femininity of women and does so by eliminating everything in the male which is not purely masculine. Others see him as simply the embodiment of latent homosexuality, hopeless love for the mother, and a fear of impotence that must be exorcised by an unending series of tests.[10]

If any of these interpretations have merit, it is because Mozart and Da Ponte approach the Don Juan myth with their own sense of freedom. The religious background of Tirso's drama does not interest them, and so they drop it. For all its supernatural byplay, the opera has no more dogma in it than Shakespeare's *Hamlet*. But when the Statue speaks with all the dreadful authority of that "other world" which in this work is neither Christian nor pagan, Mozart freely introduces the trombones that in the eighteenth century were mainly used for religious music. Similarly, *Don Giovanni* retains little of the tradition of the morality play, unlike the work of Mòlière. There is some moralizing in the opera, notably in the sententious remarks of the Epilogue, but not much of the psychological insight that fills every page of Molière's masterpiece. Don Giovanni is not introspective, and apart from the brief Credo I quoted, he scarcely tries to justify his behavior. Moving freely through the words and music, he embodies the principle of freedom without enunciating it at any length. With nothing original to sustain them but their special talent for constructing an "exotick and irrational entertainment" (as Dr. Johnson called Italian opera in general), no great and new ideas in the areas of religion or morality that pertain to the myth, Mozart and Da Ponte avail themselves of whatever comes to hand, much as Don Giovanni uses his one grand "talento" to manoeuver through the broken field of female sexuality.

As a result, *Don Giovanni* is in many ways a vulgarization, and even a diminution, of the myth. But in allowing themselves the freedom to simplify the religious and moral interests of their predecessors, Mozart and Da Ponte end up with a character who is more

---

[10]See *The Theatre of Don Juan: A Collection of Plays and Views, 1630–1963*, ed. Oscar Mandel (Lincoln: University of Nebraska Press, 1963). See also Leo Weinstein, *The Metamorphoses of Don Juan* (New York: AMS, 1967).

totally revolutionary than any of the earlier Don Juans. Alienated from church, nation, and even family, he seems to enjoy an unlimited power to give and take love with utter abandon.

The notion of a freely given love belongs to that medieval heritage from which the eighteenth century could never wholly liberate itself. Mozart and Da Ponte use the old ideas of love only as they fit into the dramatic vehicle, but they use them nonetheless. In the Middle Ages the principal concepts were those of eros and agapē. Through eros mankind sought its final good in a deity whose very nature attracted all created beings as their ultimate goal, their destination, their proper object of love. Through agapē God himself loved his creatures, bestowing upon them all the goods that sustain them in their being—and above all, the ability to love him in return.[11] Centuries before the writing of *Don Giovanni*, thinkers in the West had begun to humanize these concepts. Without denying that God was both the source of love and also the only object ultimately worthy of it, they applied the concepts of eros and agapē to love between human beings. By the eighteenth century the idea of God's love was often put in abeyance, and many freethinkers dispensed with it entirely. What remained was the concept of love as a natural force that caused men and women to discover value in one another while also creating it in the very process of love itself. Eros and agapē could thus be effectively united within the sphere of human nature alone.

It would be tempting to think of eros as typical of the masculine principle, of agapē as typical of the feminine principle, and of their wedding as a guarantee of harmony between the sexes. Attempts of this sort have been made by writers in the twentieth century such as Paul Tillich and M. C. D'Arcy. I do not think they succeed, and possibly the figure of Don Giovanni shows us why. For as the exemplar of the free and predatory male, Don Giovanni combines both eros and agapē within himself. With their wonderful sense of aesthetic license, Mozart and Da Ponte use the Don Juan myth to give their protagonist a human equivalent of both kinds of religious love. He is not, however, a loving person.

Like the devout Christian, Don Giovanni seeks his final good in a perfection that exceeds all the satisfactions of this world. For him this unattainable goal is the female sex in its totality, and though he enjoys two thousand women, or two million, his love can

[11]On this, see my book *The Nature of Love: Plato to Luther* (New York: Random House, 1966).

never be fully satisfied. Hence the theme of frustration and erotic failure leading to further pursuit, which has the same significance in this opera as it does in the theology of St. Augustine. But also Don Giovanni bestows goodness in the manner of the Christian deity. His *buon natural* radiates sexual energy as if he were indeed a fertility god. All the life in the music as well as in the plot stems from him and from his need to love. "È tutto amore," he mythically says of his behavior. This love he offers indiscriminately to all women; and within the limits of his sensuous playfulness, he uses it as a vehicle of imaginative creativity. He lavishes it on the lowly as well as the high and mighty, on the ugly as well as the beautiful, the stupid as well as the clever. As Leporello says, he gives his love freely to anyone who wears a skirt. In a sense, it is a pity that the homosexual thesis does not have more to recommend it. For then Don Giovanni could be at least bisexual, in one way or another, and thus closer in his vital bestowal to the agapastic love which the Christian God offered to all men and women.

At the same time that he humanizes the concepts of eros and agapē, Don Giovanni also makes a travesty of them. Underlying the traditional ideas about love is the assumption that it fully satisfies and does not deceive. For Don Giovanni, however, it is always the basis for dissatisfaction and ever-increasing deception. As in all the previous versions of the myth, Don Giovanni pursues the values of nature only for the sake of violating them. He probes the empirical world without lingering over the consummations it can afford. He is like the scientist who uncovers natural goods but cannot enjoy them in a life worth living. In this respect he resembles Goethe's Faust. But Faust wanted to *possess all pleasures,* and he sought for power that would enable him to fulfill his hedonic ideal. Don Giovanni has no such ambition. Despite the sybaritic moments that recur throughout the opera, he is devoted to adventure for its own sake, for sexual conquest as an end in itself. He is much more experienced than Faust, much wiser in the ways of the world, and much more pessimistic about the ideals that even a magical hedonist might espouse.

In Tirso's version of the myth, Don Juan is primarily a trickster. Mozart's Don Giovanni also plays tricks but in a way that he himself does not always recognize. His superficial allure fools him into thinking that what he does is love and nothing else. It's all love, he says, ignoring everything he does which is not love at all. In masking his activity in the guise of positive goods with which love has always been associated, he perpetrates a trick upon himself.

Dedicated to a movement that has no culmination, to a flight towards goods that never really satisfy, he is a being who freely bestows but really has little to give.

Don Giovanni is often identified with Mephistopheles. But though he must end up in hell, he is not the same character. The Devil is either positive evil or else the privation of good. Don Giovanni is neither. He expresses a whole gamut of male instincts, and he awakens those that might otherwise have slumbered in the female. In his kinship to nature and human animality, he staunchly opposes authorities that condemn what they cannot understand. And though he can never rest in any satisfaction, his deceptions are always part of a search for goodness rather than a mere privation of it. If he is a principle rather than a person, an abstraction rather than a concrete individual, as I do believe, he belongs to a different category from the Devil. He is a daemon in the Greek sense, a vital force that hovers between men and the gods, a messenger of good intent and even a messiah, but one that has lost its way in the maze of self-deception. He is the Platonic Eros but with a *core di sasso,* a "heart of stone," as Leporello says. Blocked from within as well as from without, he is somewhat pitiful despite his gaiety. We do not feel that we can judge him—he is so vibrant, so immediate, and yet so futile. He disarms our moral indignation and mesmerizes us with the dynamism of his hopeless mission. We can hardly respond to him as if he were human: we can only stare with delight and amazement. Perhaps it was this that led Kierkegaard to call Don Giovanni "the daemonic in aesthetic indifference."

5. Death and the Commendatore

As a blocked principle of vitality, Don Giovanni is suitably contrasted with the Statue of the Commendatore. As the former is not the Devil, neither is the other a saint or ministering angel. In Tirso and Molière, the Commendatore is one among several father-figures whose authority Don Juan systematically challenges. In Mozart, however, there are no fathers other than the Commendatore. He alone must therefore represent the social order, the moral status quo that Don Giovanni violates. The opera begins with a duel between these contrary principles and ends with a violent reversal of the earlier outcome. The Commendatore has no being otherwise, at least not dramatically. Though he is the other kind of man to which I referred, he is not a person. He functions in the opera as merely a negative response to Don Giovanni's demand for freedom. He signifies everything in society that restrains sexual *libertà*. Where the fathers in Tirso and Molière are individuals whose personality (generally a mixture of virtue and vice) helps us to understand the rebellious truancy of Don Juan, Mozart's Commendatore is just a pasteboard abstraction who fights for his daughter's honor and then becomes a hair-raising deus ex machina.

If Don Giovanni is blocked vitality, the Commendatore is death-in-life—the dead come to life, not being twice-born like Christ but arresting natural impulses it considers evil. We know that the myth was originally composed of two elements: one, the theme of the rake's progress; the other, the story of the stone guest, the statue or cadaver who invites a man to visit the dead and then will not let him return to the living.[12] The latter theme fills many a medieval drama, death appearing at the feast, skeletons luring men into their tombs, the dead preying upon the quick, and worms feeding on both. Since they do not develop the moral and religious significance of the myth, Mozart and Da Ponte come closer to the old legend of the stone guest than either Tirso or Molière. Da Ponte modelled his libretto upon the opera of Gazzaniga and Bertati entitled *Don Giovanni Tenorio o sia Il Convitato di Pietra*, which not only gives the stone guest equal billing in the title but also indicates how the legend was taken in the eighteenth century. Bertati's libretto deals with the affairs of an opera company that reluctantly decides to perform the Don Juan story. They justify their choice of what they consider to be such a tasteless plot by sadly reasoning that the noise and clamor of it all will bring in the groundlings.[13]

In Mozart's treatment of the Commendatore, the same attitude survives. He uses the idea of the stone guest quite dramatically, but also in a jocular manner. As a daemon of life, Don Giovanni must be countered by a daemon of death. The Statue performs that service admirably. At the end it takes revenge for the murder in the first scene, thereby enabling both acts to be organized about the conflict between vitality and petrification. The

[12]See John Austen, *The Story of Don Juan: A Study of the Legend and the Hero* (London: Secker, 1939).

[13]For a discussion of this and other forerunners of Mozart's opera, see Giovanni Macchia, *Vita, aventure e morte di Don Giovanni* (Bari: Editori Laterza, 1966), pp. 73-111. See also Edward J. Dent, *Mozart's Operas* (London: Oxford University Press, 1960), pp. 129-33.

great ensemble which ends the first act not only reveals Don Giovanni eluding his pursuers once again, but also prepares us for the moment of dead reckoning when he will not be able to escape. The music strongly anticipates the visitation of the Statue, and the repeated references to thunderbolts prepare us for the noisy descent into hellfire. All of this commands attention as it should; and since Don Giovanni is the defender of male sensuousness, it is entirely appropriate for his running music to be balanced, even outdone, by sensationalistic effects at the end of both acts.

But though the Commendatore and his statue prefigure death-in-life, it would be a mistake to study them for doctrinal implications. They do not signify any special allegiance to hell-fire religion or hidebound morality. The stone guest symbolizes death, and Mozart's music makes us feel the horror of it, but an operatic statue that nods its head and clambers into the dining hall cannot serve as the basis for theological commitment. The stone guest's fearful music merely expresses the terror that death inspires. There is no reason to think that either Mozart or his eighteenth-century audiences took it as anything else.

Tirso's Don Juan is a Catholic awaiting God's condemnation; Molière's is a freethinker eager to investigate all possibilities. But the Don Giovanni of Mozart and Da Ponte is essentially frivolous—like the sensuous itself. He believes in nothing that goes beyond his superficial senses. In the graveyard, he suspects a fraud, and he is sure of it when the Statue utters banalities about avenging himself on the man who killed him in a duel. When Don Giovanni now calls the Statue a *vecchio buffonissimo*—a "big old clown"—he speaks for the audience as well as for himself. Possibly his remark relieves that fear of the unknown which the thought of the dead always occasions, as when Hamlet tries to compose himself by addressing his father's ghost as "truepenny" and "old mole." But it also enables us to see that even the destruction of human vitality may be jocular as well as dramatic, and therefore absurd.

The humor of it all appears in Leporello's every response to the incredible phenomenon of the lifelike Statue. How can one mistake the farcical playacting in both music and text when the servant, being prodded by the sword of a master who threatens to bury him on the spot (since they are in a graveyard), addresses the somehow living, somehow dead piece of marble with these sonorous words: "O statua gent*ilissima*"? Don Giovanni laughs and so do we. "What fun!" he says. "What a joke!" And when the monument

44

comes to dinner later on, how can we take the proceedings as having doctrinal importance when Leporello imitates the Statue's gait—"ta, ta, ta, ta!"—hides under the table, keeps telling us how much he is shaking, and advises his master to decline the return invitation on the grounds that he is too busy at the moment! Don Giovanni rejects Leporello's advice. As always, he plays the game. This one has rules he does not understand, but despite the loud trombones he is right to consider it a test of strength rather than the revelation of metaphysical reality.

For this reason, critics who treat *Don Giovanni* as evidence of Catholic sentiments in Mozart have missed the point entirely. Brigid Brophy sees deep ambivalences in the fact that the hero ends up in a state of damnation even though Mozart, as a newly initiated Mason, no longer believed in such dogmas.[14] But though Mozart and Da Ponte *could* have eliminated the supernatural baggage of the original story, their retaining it does not indicate a theological design. Goldoni was so offended by the stone guest crudities of the legend that he dispensed with them entirely. Mozart and Da Ponte did not find this necessary. Far from endorsing a system of beliefs, they magnify everything—music, words, and general harum scarum—so grotesquely that nothing in it can ever be used to assert religious ideas of any interest.

If Mozart had really been ambivalent about his Catholic origins, he would have developed in the Commendatore a plausible psychology contrary to Don Giovanni's. He attempts nothing of the sort. The Commendatore has his being only in death—his own at the beginning of the opera and Don Giovanni's at the end. His role is merely the presenting of obstacles to unlicensed vitality. So little did the Statue inspire Mozart with positive possibilities that he even steals some of its music from Gluck. With the same voice that the Oracle in *Alceste* uses to say, "Il re morrà / s'altrui per lui non more" ("The king will die unless someone else dies for him"), Mozart has the Statue announce his arrival for dinner. Was he consciously parodying the awesomeness of Gluck? I would not rule that out. Like Don Giovanni, Mozart was himself a notorious prankster. And as one who had also rejected the traditional dogma, he would have had little reason to exempt it from the mocking gibes of *dramma giocoso*.

[14]Brigid Brophy, *Mozart the Dramatist* (New York: Harcourt, Brace, & World, 1964), p. 203.

45

6. Leporello's Dream

If Don Giovanni and the Commendatore balance each other as abstract principles, a daemonic search for sexual freedom checked by death-in-life, Leporello is nevertheless a real person. Among the men at least, he is virtually the only person in this opera; and perhaps it can all be taken as his private fantasy, like the dream of H. C. E. in *Finnegans Wake*.[15] In Shaw it is Tanner who dreams of himself as Don Juan in Hell, and he learns that hell is just the life of sensuous pleasure. In Mozart's opera the sensuous is the predominant realm of being; and Leporello moves through it like one who expects at every moment to be awakened by some repressive reality. But somehow the dream goes on. At the end of the opera, when Leporello must look for a new master, he hastens to the local inn— the most likely place to find another libertine. We may be sure that his new life will be a continuation of the old one.

The opera begins with Leporello pacing nervously, waiting outside while his master makes love; it ends with Leporello as the sole survivor of their escapades. In between, he participates in the action as much as Don Giovanni himself. Far from being a mere servant, he is always an intimate part of everything that happens. He does not manipulate the action, like Figaro, but his presence is absolutely essential. In treating love as a game, Don Giovanni must have an audience on stage as well as in the theatre. Leporello fills that role. He is our representative; and though we feel superior to him, we find it easy to put ourselves in his place. Once we do that, we see that Don Giovanni's pursuit of women is really a communal hunt masquerading as a game. Don Giovanni in the moonlight says the night seems made "per gir a zonzo a caccia di ragazze"—"for strolling about on a girl-hunt." He and Leporello are partners in the chase, one standing guard while the other attacks, each performing a job within a joint activity. Leporello is the lesser member of the team, but otherwise not wholly different from his master. He has similar tastes in sex and enjoys having Donna Elvira fling her arms about him much as Don Giovanni would. He likes the idea of deceiving her. For though he commiserates with Elvira while he is a mere observer, the moment he starts participating he tells us that the joke—"la burla"—suits him very well.

Indeed, what else does Leporello want other than to become

---

[15] In *Mozart on the Stage* (New York: Coward-McCann, 1947), Christopher Benn also suggests that the whole of *Don Giovanni* may be regarded as Leporello's dream.

Don Giovanni himself? In his first appearance, while pacing back and forth, he says that he too wants to play the gentleman, to let someone else be the sentinel while *he* stays inside with a beautiful woman. He wants to be the leader of the hunt, the spearthrower for once and not a mere lookout. In changing garments with him, Don Giovanni gives Leporello his big opportunity. But instead of profiting from it, he scarcely knows what to do with Elvira; and when he rejoins his master, he complains that the adventure nearly got him killed, as if there were nothing in it that he could enjoy. Obviously, Leporello is incapable of taking over the principal function. He is a born follower. This does not prevent him from dreaming of leadership and grumbling about his fate, but it means that at the moment of truth—either in embracing a woman or in facing death—he cannot rise to the occasion. He is therefore comically impotent and need not be punished, unlike his more competent master.

Otto Rank speaks of Leporello as the animistic "double" of Don Giovanni and even his conscience.[16] This may apply remotely to Sganarelle in Molière, but it is certainly not true of Leporello. Though he criticizes Don Giovanni once or twice, he rarely speaks with the voice of conscience. Unlike Sganarelle he never enters into a moral debate of any significance. And neither is he Don Giovanni's double, any more than we in the audience are. As ordinary persons, we may approximate but we cannot embody an abstract principle of sexuality in the way that Don Giovanni does. Leporello fails in his approximation because that other abstraction—the deadly Commendatore—frightens and immobilizes him. Observing the duel in the first act and the duellike confrontation at the end, Leporello is petrified by the conflict between life and death. He temporizes not because he flourishes in time and loves its ephemeral passage, as Don Giovanni does, but because he is waiting to see which principle will win out.

When death does, as indeed it must, Leporello gleefully joins the other characters in the moralistic Epilogue. Like them, he celebrates the just punishment of that terrible rogue Don Giovanni. But earlier he sang a different tune entirely in explaining the famous catalogue to Donna Elvira. And one can well imagine

[16]*The Don Juan Legend,* trans. and ed. with an introduction by David G. Winter (Princeton: Princeton University Press, 1975), pp. 45-52. See also Otto Rank, *The Double,* trans. and ed. Harry Tucker, Jr. (Chapel Hill: University of North Carolina Press, 1971).

Leporello keeping the list for his own amusement. As a daemonic and universal male, Don Giovanni has too vast a perspective to worry about itemization. He directs himself to all women in general. Leporello himself says that "every home, every village, every town can testify to his amorous undertakings." For women are all subject to the attentions of some predatory male or other, who, lumped together as an abstraction, may very well be personified as Don Giovanni. But it is only a Leporello, with his bureaucratic mentality, who makes a list of individual females; and it is only he who gloats over the number of names on it.

Mille e tre! In Spain alone there are already a thousand and three! But why should the number make any difference? Is a thousand and three any better than a thousand and two? Only to Leporello, for he is out of it all and can understand success in love or sex merely by its prurient quantification. While Don Giovanni yearns for an impossible infinity, Leporello thinks only about an ever-increasing sum. Don Giovanni dazzles women by making each feel that she is uniquely desirable, which she is to him at that moment, but Leporello puts them into classified groups as if they were so many commodities: country women, city women, chambermaids, countesses, baronesses, marchionesses, princesses, rich and poor, ugly and beautiful, women of every rank, of every age, of every shape. For Leporello they only exist as names on a list that he unrolls into an audience that scans it for the local favorites. He does all this to prove to Elvira that she will be neither the first one nor the last, and therefore that she ought to bow submissively to the mere force of numbers. Don Giovanni would never say this or even think it. When Elvira catches him with Zerlina, he honestly admits to his purely sensuous interests: "I want to amuse myself." But Leporello has to clothe the empirical fact with the comfort and assurance of a mathematical platitude. "The square is not round!" he tells Elvira. *He* is the one whose religion is arithmetic.

The catalogue aria tells us something about Mozart as well as Da Ponte. When Leporello shows his "non picciol libro" to Elvira, three suggestive notes on the harpsichord show him flipping through the pages or glancing at the scroll as a way of tantalizing the poor woman. As he begins to sing about the list, the strings start dancing light-heartedly at the prospect of such merciless merriment. They seem to be skipping around Elvira, taunting her with the mere existence of this not-small book. Before long the entire orchestra is rollicking with laughter, snorting and almost whistling in appreciation of the sexual hero who conquers one female after another. In the course of the aria, the supporting music expresses glory and pride mingled with comic incredulity. Mozart understands Leporello's mentality, and here at least, he responds unambiguously as a fellow male who savors the chauvinistic display.

In explicating his catalogue, Leporello uses Da Ponte's classical education to parody the attack upon the deceitfulness of love which Lucretius introduces into *De Rerum Natura*. "With blondes it is his custom to praise their gentleness," Leporello says, "with brunettes their constancy, with white-haired ones their sweetness. In winter he wants plumpness; in summer he wants leanness. The tall woman is stately; the tiny girl is always charming." In Lucretius the comparable passage describes, with much consternation, how lovers deceive themselves. But when Ovid wrote his variations on the same text, he did so as a way of teaching men how to deceive the women they pursue. Leporello is doing neither one nor the other. He describes Don Giovanni's habits in the hope that Elvira will lose heart and go away without bothering them any more. Like Ovid, however, he also envies a seducer's artfulness with language. He admires Don Giovanni's imagination. As all men do, he wishes that he too could find so fertile a means of enjoying each and every woman. Earlier in the eighteenth century, Dr. Johnson had said: "Were it not for imagination, Sir, a man would be as happy in the arms of a chambermaid as of a Duchess." Dr. Johnson did not seem to realize that one requires imagination in order to be happy in the arms of either. Don Giovanni has it in abundance, and he enjoys *both* the duchess and the chambermaid, using each as a different occasion for sensuous pleasure.

Even the old ones can satisfy his master, Leporello says, if only to give him the wicked delight of knowing they can be had. And of course, there are the virgins; but then Leporello sings of them with a bit of hesitation. He almost slurs over the lines "Sua passion predominante / È la giovin principiante" ("his predominant passion is for the young beginner"). Don Juan may have started his mythic career as a medicine man, an itinerant healer who also practiced ritual defloration.[17] In reaction against the Christian idea that virginity was a state of holiness, libertines in the eighteenth century often sought to carry out defloration as a rite subversive to the ruling ideology. But in Leporello's catalogue, the young beginner is

---

[17]On this, see Sigmund Freud, "The Taboo of Virginity," in *Sexuality and the Psychology of Love* (New York: Collier Books, 1963). This essay is one of Freud's three "Contributions to the Psychology of Love," available in various editions.

just one among many types of women. The aria uses the phrase only once, as if to hurry past the unwholesome implications of this particular activity. Given the text, Mozart could have repeated the words many times. He calls for repetition at various other places in the catalogue, and one might have thought that Don Giovanni's *passion predominante* would receive special attention, whatever it might be. It is interesting that Mozart protects his sensuous hero in this regard, though he will not go so far as to delete the phrase. In his book on Mozart, Alfred Einstein says in passing that "but for Mozart, this aria would never have contained the two lines about innocence betrayed, which are spoken to an uncanny *pianissimo.*"[18] One must assume that Mozart realized that so shocking a concept required only a single, muted expression. He saw that delicacy here would be more effective than emphasis.

Leporello ends his account by reminding Elvira that anyhow *she* knows what Don Giovanni does—"voi sapete quel che fa." Yes, she does. That is why she, and all the others, can never get enough of him. On the word *fa* Mozart has Leporello repeat the vowel sound as if he were both laughing at Elvira and also insinuating that she is just as naughty as his master. She acted knowingly: why should she complain? So he seems to be saying.[19] But also, Leporello laughs because he is external to a situation that he can neither duplicate nor understand. His laughter is a titter of embarrassment, not merely a final insult to Elvira, as it is usually interpreted. In the last analysis, only a woman can appreciate the daemonic charm of a Don Giovanni. In his sexual banality, the ordinary man sniggers at it. Before one who has herself experienced the sacrament, he can only bow out nervously. And in fact, at this point Leporello runs away.

7. Don Giovanni's Power over Women

Though Leporello escapes the issue, we must stay and face it. What is the secret charm of Don Giovanni? What is it about women that causes them to succumb? Kierkegaard thought that "the true expression of woman consists in her desire to be seduced"—an

[18]Alfred Einstein, *Mozart: His Character, His Work* (London: Oxford University Press, 1945), pp. 438–39.
[19]On this and other details of the aria, see Charles Gounod, *Mozart's Don Giovanni: A Commentary* (New York: Da Capo Press, 1970), pp. 24–32.

extraordinary remark, and one that sounds foreign to the world we now live in. But even if Kierkegaard were right, one would want to know why women desire to be seduced by Don Giovanni. Is it the gaiety and glamor that he exudes throughout the opera? Or the fact that he affords sorrows as well as joy, and thereby makes boredom impossible? Or possibly his reputation alone, his sheer publicity, so that it becomes shameful *not* to be on the list—as if one were too ugly or undesirable?

Don Giovanni's technique shows itself in his unctuous promises to Zerlina, but the phenomenology behind it appears more graphically in the serenade *Deh vieni alla finestra*. Alfred de Musset found a mocking disparity between the words and the music of the serenade, the text being trite and overly earnest while the accompaniment dances merrily on the mandoline.[20] Though this is true, and though we know from the sound of the sensuous music that, whatever he says, Don Giovanni is only playacting, the words of his serenade are worth considering in themselves. For they indicate what some women want to hear—at least, women in the eighteenth century who were susceptible to this kind of man. "Come, come to the window, oh my treasure, come, come to console my tears. If you refuse to give me some relief, I will die before your eyes! You have a mouth sweeter than honey, you who bring sweetness to the depths of my heart! Do not be cruel with me, my joy! At least let yourself be seen, my beautiful love!"

Appearing on the page like this, and in English, the sentiments are sufficiently outrageous to make us wonder who could respond to them. Perhaps they are suitable only for a silly maidservant or a ninny like Zerlina. Perhaps that is why Mozart gave the serenade that lively melody, not only to mock at the preposterous language but also to poke fun at any woman who could be seduced by it. And yet, the sentiments are those that troubadours and trouvères had been singing to good effect—both erotically and poetically—for five or six hundred years. Don Giovanni has obviously read Bernard de Ventadour, Petrarch, Ronsard, and all the others who find a treasure in their beloved, who beg her to console their tears, who feel themselves wounded by the lady's eyes and threaten to expire in her sight, who describe her as a delicacy whose very words are made of honey, who beg her not to be cruel, and who end by pleading for nothing but a few innocent pleasures (mainly visual).

What could be more *charming*, in the sense of an enchantment,

---

[20]*Namouna*, I, XIV, and XV. See Weinstein, *Metamorphoses of Don Juan*, p. 59n.

than these conceits? While awakening the woman's sensibility, they make no assault upon her senses. They are as sensuous as a breeze in Monteverdi's madrigals, or lapping water in Botticelli's *Birth of Venus*. The voice caresses and touches the lady at a distance. Though it speaks of passion, its sound is too melodious for that. Without endangering the woman in any way, it flatters her and calms her fear of the aggressive male. For how dangerous can he be, standing there foreshadowed by her elevation on the balcony, wooing her with a mandoline instead of a dagger? The more ludicrous the poetry, the greater its effectiveness. She knows he will not die *whatever* she does, but in talking that way he seems to renounce the usual male demands, pretends to be incapable of dominating, and so dramatically enacts the sexual submission that everyone knows he will eventually expect of her. His apparent weakness, his attestation of distress, his begging her to relieve him in any manner that she will, hypnotically suggests what is to happen to the woman herself. By dignifying the notion of surrender, it all encourages the woman to yield. If the nice young man is already seduced, why should she not be? The music makes it seem harmless, effortless, and gay. Moreover, he sings beautifully and therefore must be capable in various ways.

For Don Giovanni such serenades are but a trick within the game. He masquerades as a troubadour because he knows that every servant girl would like to play the haughty lady. He succeeds as often as he does because (like the troubadours, many of whom were also Don Juans) he knows one great truth about female sexuality. Though it is wrong to say that women want to be seduced, Don Giovanni knows they will gladly give themselves to someone they admire and think they can love. He also knows that they fear this inclination and will fight it less vigorously with a man who seems helpless in his need for what only women can give.

And who could act this out better than Don Giovanni? His life is an eternal dependency upon women. He knows at first hand their strengths and weaknesses. From long experience he has learned how to mask his sexual aggressiveness by an appearance of passivity that was generally expected of women in the western world. As women have always considered themselves to be what Simone de Beauvoir calls "the slaves of nature," Don Giovanni seduces them into thinking that he is the slave to *their* nature. At the same time he also acts like an aristocrat, a successful man among men, one who has earned the right to dominate.

This play between aggression and submission in the male is an aspect of sensuousness itself. Don Giovanni can intrigue the female because he intuitively knows that she often experiences something similar. Treacherous though he may be, women sense his ambivalence and identify it with elements in their own character. They are equally capable of seducing sensuously, and they often dominate while appearing to submit. Despite his dubious anthropology, the French novelist Choderlos de Laclos spoke of women in a way that corroborates Don Giovanni's attunement to the ones he knows. In a remarkable essay on the education of women written in 1783, just four years before the opera, Laclos describes the original enslavement of women and then their eventual emancipation through sex: "They felt at last that the only resource of the weak was to seduce; they learned that if they were dependent on men because of their weakness, they could make these same men dependent on them by pleasure. Less fortunate than men, they had to think and reflect the more. They it was who first knew that pleasure never comes so high as the idea one may form of it, and that imagination goes farther than nature. With these prime truths in hand, they learned first to veil their charms and arouse curiosity. They practised the painful art of refusal, even when they wished to consent: with that they discovered how to fire the imagination of men, how to call forth and direct desire. And thus beauty and love were born."[21]

Mozart could not have read these words, but it is as if Laclos had Don Giovanni in mind when he then says: "Sometimes, too, men have turned against women the arms which the women had forged to fight men, and then the slavery of women is more abject than ever." One might apply this to the myth as a whole, but it seems especially appropriate to Mozart's version. There is something female about the beauty of sensuous music. We associate the male with trumpet calls and military marches. When Don Giovanni mesmerizes his prey by singing sweetly, as in his serenade, we feel he must have learned the art from women. The fact that he is a baritone, rather than a light tenor like Don Ottavio, merely accentuates the effect. It makes him that much more beguiling, though also more insidious.

Since Don Giovanni dominates throughout the opera, the slavery of women to which Laclos refers becomes a major theme. It is basic to any understanding of Donna Anna, Donna Elvira, and Zerlina. They struggle for their freedom, but they attain it only

[21]"On the Education of Woman," reprinted as Appendix 4 of Wayland Young, *Eros Denied: Sex in Western Society* (New York: Grove Press, 1966), pp. 349–50.

imperfectly, and Mozart systematically prevents their militant consciousness from appearing heroic. The women respond to their enslaved condition in ways that debase them more than in any other version of the myth. Confronted with the spectacle of a cunning and deceitful male, we should not have found it too hard to sympathize with his victims. Yet this rarely happens in Mozart's opera. It is never easy to feel moral indignation while listening to great music; but even so, the female characters in *Don Giovanni* are filled with so much hatred and vocal violence that we soon find ourselves shocked into neutrality.

From her very first line, in which she calls Don Giovanni "quel barbaro," Donna Elvira sounds like a woman that *any* husband would leave behind. She is much more than that, as I will suggest; but if every woman were like her, one could more easily appreciate Don Giovanni's desire to escape them all. Of Donna Anna one sees little other than her sheer vindictiveness. She does assure Don Ottavio that she loves him and will someday be his wife, but in the drama she appears mainly as a persecuting harpy. And Zerlina shows such insensitivity towards Masetto while the fit for Don Giovanni is on her that one feels that nothing the seducer would do to her could possibly balance the scales. In a scene Mozart added for the Vienna performance but which is rarely included nowadays, Zerlina menaces Leporello with a razor and threatens to cut out his hair, his head, his heart, and his eyes. She ties his hands until the ropes hurt, shouting all the while that she is a furious tigress, an asp, a lioness. "I feel my breast burning with joy and delight! Thus, thus one acts with men, thus, thus," etc. As against women like that, how humane and civilized Don Giovanni appears in dispensing his natural goodness. One only wonders why he bothers.

Why does Mozart go out of his way, as it seems, to make the female characters so ferocious? All of the passionate music in the opera belongs to them, and it is always the passion of angry and wounded women. In that essay from which I quoted, Rolland claims that the only passions Mozart knew well were anger and pride. These are not pleasant emotions, and they contradict traditional attitudes about the nature of love. In giving them to the women in *Don Giovanni,* Mozart makes the warfare of the sexes equally ugly on both sides. The women are passionate but filled with hatred, and the sexually dominant male only pretends to be passionate in love. He has made the sensuous life into a passion, but he is never passionate about another person. Only his pursuers are, the women he has conquered by enacting a native sensuousness which they may also have but will never be able to enjoy.

8. The Sorrows of Donna Anna

Among these three violent females, Donna Anna has given the critics the most trouble. She does not appear in Molière; but in Tirso she serves as a woman who has possibly been seduced, even raped, by Don Juan. The last part of the play largely concerns itself with the question of her honor, and just before he dies Don Juan informs the world that he did not succeed with her. With this in mind, many critics have assumed that Mozart and Da Ponte created their Donna Anna as an operatic version of Tirso's. But there is no reason to believe that they did, and any number of difficulties evaporate if we take Donna Anna as a new creation. She resembles Tirso's Ana in admitting the Don into her presence late at night because she thinks he is her lover Ottavio, in spurning Don Giovanni's overtures, in having a father whom Don Giovanni kills in a duel and who kills Don Giovanni after returning as a statue. Otherwise, Mozart's Anna is another character entirely. For though she enters the action as a woman Don Giovanni has tried to seduce, she remains as the daughter of the slain Commendatore.

Once we make this shift in our critical perspective, everything else falls into place. Why is Anna so vindictive, so bloodthirsty in her pursuit of the intruder although so frail a person that she nearly faints two or three times in the course of the opera? Why does she delay Don Ottavio although she claims to love him and never once denies that she will marry him one day? Possibly because of the sexual shock. Some critics say that she has indeed been raped, despite her assuring Don Ottavio to the contrary. Einstein claims that Don Giovanni "has reached the summit of his desires" with her.[22] Another writer insists that she "has just enjoyed a passionate love-affair with Don Giovanni."[23] But it seems much more plausible to see her as a dutiful daughter both grief-stricken and embittered by the death of her father. Since he died fighting for her honor, killed by the man she admitted into her bed-

[22]*Mozart,* p. 439.
[23]Moberly, *Three Mozart Operas,* p. 151. See also Pierre Jean Jouve, *Mozart's Don Juan,* trans. Eric Earnshaw Smith (London: Vincent Stuart, 1957), p. 24, where we are told that Donna Anna, "attached by an unconscious fixation to her father, has transferred to Don Juan her desire to be seduced, to be raped."

chamber, one might relate her anger to feelings of guilt for having involved her father in her own nocturnal adventures. But we need not go that far, and surely what matters most in the opera is Anna's grief for a lost parent rather than any intimacy she may have had with Don Giovanni. She seeks to avenge her father just as her father had sought to avenge her. When she and Don Ottavio fail to act quickly enough, the Commendatore intervenes a second time.

In his book on Mozart's operas, Dent argues that Donna Anna and Don Ottavio "were evidently intended by Da Ponte to be the pair of more or less serious lovers customary in most Italian comic operas."[24] This being so, it seems quite normal for Donna Anna to ask Don Ottavio to wait the conventional year before they get married. There is no reason to think she harbors a secret love for Don Giovanni or finds him superior to Don Ottavio. For that matter, there is little cause for anyone to vilify Don Ottavio—as so many critics have in the last two hundred years. E. T. A. Hoffmann describes him as follows: "He is a delicate, overdressed fop of twenty-one at most. Being Anna's bridegroom, he probably lives in the house, since he could be summoned so swiftly; he could have rushed to the scene to save the old man at the initial sounds of combat, but he first had to spruce up. Besides, he was none too anxious to venture out into the night."[25]

This is all fabrication, of course. Don Ottavio is the conventional suitor, but he is not a fop or coward. He has no place in the duel scene any more than in the visitation of the stone guest. It is not an opera about him or his kind of man. He is primarily a bit of stage-furniture, a human prop for the ballerina—in this case, Anna as a daughter who requires a substitute for her father and as a woman who will someday need a husband. Given this function, Don Ottavio plays his part quite well. He supports Anna, tracks down the intruder, confronts Don Giovanni, and finally takes the matter to the proper authorities.

In one way or another, Ottavio is a frustrated male throughout the opera and therefore an adequate contrast to the fabulous seducer—whose final frustration clears the way for Don Ottavio's success. Like Don Giovanni at his subtlest, Don Ottavio sings with

[24]Dent, *Mozart's Operas,* p. 157.

[25]"Don Juan," as quoted and translated in Weinstein, *Metamorphoses of Don Juan,* pp. 56–57. For the complete text in two alternative translations, cf. E. T. A. Hoffmann, "Don Juan," in *Tales of Hoffmann,* ed. Christopher Lazare (New York: A. A. Wyn, 1946), and E. T. A. Hoffmann, "A Tale of Don Juan," in *Pleasures of Music,* ed. Jacques Barzun.

all the sweetness of a troubadour. But where Don Giovanni is sensuous and nothing else, Don Ottavio would seem to feel that passionate yearning for the beloved which the troubadours introduced into western literature. In him, however, it is faint and rather feeble, diluted by rococo courtesy, denatured by too many civilized conventions. Here again, Mozart refuses to accord the male anything like the strong passion which his females so easily enjoy in their moments of anger and indignation. In fact, Don Ottavio is weaker than any of his counterparts in the earlier versions of the myth. He is a gentle man who can hardly compete with the strong, commanding voice of Don Giovanni. He serves by standing and waiting until Mozart throws some lovely aria in his direction. Except for the duet *Che giuramento, o dei!* in which Donna Anna gets him to join her in swearing vengeance, Mozart never gives Ottavio music that is at all heroic. To this extent, one can see why Donna Anna might have preferred a virile and forceful male such as Don Giovanni. But that possibility is never developed in the opera, and therefore her passion cannot be explained as thwarted sexual desire.

In being the dutiful but guilt-ridden child who seeks to redeem her lost parent, Donna Anna oddly reminds us of Mozart's own condition. Otto Rank thought that the conflict between Don Giovanni and the Statue, as well as the ambivalence between comic and tragic elements in the music, manifested feelings in Mozart that stemmed from his father's death.[26] This is always possible, particularly when one considers that in Tirso and Molière the Commendatore represents a class of authorities towards whom Mozart had very mixed sentiments. In the opera itself, the Commendatore appears primarily as Donna Anna's father, and only remotely as a social entity. But if Mozart had ambivalent feelings about his own father, they might well have been expressed through the grief and violence of Donna Anna. As one who dared to be creative, to be free in his art, and even (occasionally) to spurn repressive conventions, Mozart resembled Don Giovanni. The secrets of his love-life do not concern me at the moment, but only the fact that he did take liberties with the universe. He might therefore expect to be destroyed by the brute restraints that countercheck each act of freedom and creativity—not only death but also those powers and dominions, duties and responsibilities, that jealously administer our lives. His father was one of these controlling forces,

[26]*The Don Juan Legend*, p. 125. See also Brophy, *Mozart the Dramatist*, pp. 235ff.

and himself had died that year. In identifying with Donna Anna, Mozart could express his own feelings of filial devotion while also disclaiming too close an association with the unbounded virility that he loved so much. All this he might do by creating great music, which is what his father's rigid authority demanded in the first place. Like Donna Anna, Mozart would thus issue out of the dark night of death and into the peacefulness of a happy resolution.

If this interpretation is right, perhaps it can explain why Donna Anna's aria *Or sai chi l'onore* comes through as *opera seria* at its best, an emotional declamation without a hint of parody or comic ambiguity. This is one of the arias that Kierkegaard wanted to delete as being "really concert numbers rather than dramatic music, since, on the whole, Ottavio and Anna are far too insignificant to justify their retarding the action."[27] Kierkegaard obviously did not perceive the importance of Donna Anna. Mozart identifies with her (in a way that he does not identify with Elvira, for instance); and once we realize this, we can also see why he escapes the aesthetic failings that Berlioz imputes to him. In his *Memoirs,* Berlioz says of Donna Anna's final aria *Non mi dir:* "It is an aria of intense sadness, full of a heartbreaking sense of loss and sorrowing love, but towards the end degenerating without warning into music of such appalling inanity and vulgarity that one can hardly believe it to be the work of the same man. One has the impression that Donna Anna has suddenly dried her tears and broken out in ribald clowning. . . . Mozart in this passage has committed one of the most odious and idiotic crimes against passion, taste and common sense of which the history of art provides an example."[28]

Berlioz is objecting to the artificiality of the coloratura passage, which strikes him as both undramatic and inauthentic. To me, however, the aria, and the little scene in which it occurs, seems extremely effective. The scene appears just before the end of the opera. It is the only one in the second act that takes place by day. And indeed daylight is now beginning to return for the conventional lovers. The world of ordinary human relations is about to reassert itself, as it finally does in the Epilogue. The nocturnal vitality of Don Giovanni is soon to be dissipated. It has all been a nightmare, but now that the police have been notified, the sun shines into Donna Anna's sitting room as Don Ottavio tries to calm her down. The music is quite calm throughout the scene. Donna

[27]*Either/Or,* p. 124.
[28]*The Memoirs of Hector Berlioz,* trans. and ed. David Cairns (New York: A. A. Knopf, 1969), p. 93.

Anna's aria is not "heartbreaking," as Berlioz says. Instead, it shows Donna Anna trying to calm the torment in Don Ottavio, which she has created by postponing their wedding. The verb *calmare* occurs five times in their brief exchange.

In telling Don Ottavio why she finds it hard to quiet her nerves, Donna Anna first reminds him of her father's death. Neither the capture of Don Giovanni nor the comfort of Ottavio's love can eliminate the sadness she feels. When Ottavio says she is *crudele* (cruel) to him, Anna enters upon the recitative and aria that Berlioz finds so offensive. Now, *crudele* is the word that Renaissance masques often used for women who resisted the blandishments of their courtly lovers. In his serenade to Elvira's servant, Don Giovanni begged her not to be cruel with him in this sense. Underlying the specialized meaning, there also lingers a masculine fear of total rejection by the female. In trying to pacify Ottavio, Donna Anna insists that she loves him as much as ever and has no intention of deserting him. Since she is still a stock figure of the beloved, however, she cannot help slipping into the traditional courtly language. Thus, as the courtly lover says that he will die unless the woman reciprocates his love—this also occurs in Don Giovanni's serenade—so too the lady replies that she will die unless he restrains his impetuous demands. By reestablishing this courtly communication, Donna Anna effects a return to the normalcy of their relationship as daytime aristocrats. The references to death remind us that she is still her father's daughter, but the overall effect may very well calm the anxiety of Don Ottavio.

Beginning with "Forse, forse un giorno," the music becomes hopeful, sustaining, and even confident about the future. Far from being ribald clowning, the coloratura devices (actually quite restrained and ladylike) give us reason to think that heaven *will* provide that merciful peace which Anna seeks. The passage starts with a lilting expression of hope in the words *forse, forse* ("perhaps, perhaps"), and then weds this with the concept of *pietà*, the heavenly pity that washes away all sadness and allows one to enjoy the sunshine of a mutual love. Dramatically, not just vocally, the coloratura music is quite convincing. How could Berlioz have misconstrued it so completely?

9. The Charms of Zerlina

In relation to Don Ottavio, Donna Anna is the fleeing female. Don Ottavio pursues her as Don Giovanni pursues all women before running away from them. And like Don Giovanni, he is thwarted by the lingering influence of the Commendatore—who survives his death not only in becoming a living statue but also in his daughter's self-imposed petrifaction. At the opposite end of the social scale, Masetto pursues Zerlina much as Ottavio pursues Anna, and with the same goal of conventional matrimony. But the Commendatore's powers do not extend this far. When Zerlina repulses Masetto, which she does only for a day or two as if to tease him into shape, she acts out of a principle quite different from the one symbolized by the Commendatore. For deep down she belongs to the camp of Don Giovanni. She is a match for him, not in the sense that she escapes his domination, which she may or may not, but rather in being labile in her sentiments just as he is inconstant in his lovemaking.

Masetto complains that it is shameless for Zerlina to flirt with another man on their wedding day. But to her, all men are sex objects, and all moments of time equally transient. Since she can and will deceive Masetto whenever she wishes, why not establish the practice by enacting it at the ceremonial beginning of their marriage? Like Odette in Proust, she knows that the more she is fickle with Masetto, the more he will become jealous; the more he is jealous, the more he will dote on her; the more he dotes on her, the greater her freedom to deceive him. "Thus one acts with men." The technique is modelled upon Don Giovanni's, but turned inside out to meet the special needs of a beast that hunts by being pursued. Adelina Patti, and other great sopranos too, played Zerlina as if she were a cute and innocent girl. Even the prestigious critic Hanslick thought that "the pert little village coquette, Zerlina, becomes absolutely angelic."[29] They might do better to have seen her as a primitive minx, a gypsy, a lightweight Carmen. She lends herself to this interpretation as well as the more flattering one preferred in the nineteenth century.

In what actually occurs on stage, Zerlina is the only woman that Don Giovanni woos, apart from the serenade to Elvira's servant. It is relevant that Zerlina and the servant are both members of the lower orders. Since the peasant scenes take place in the countryside "near Don Giovanni's castle," his interest in Zerlina (or even the servant—in a sense, his wife's maid) can easily be amalgamated with Count Almaviva's attempt to seduce Susanna in *Figaro*. But *Don*

[29]Quoted in *The Mozart Handbook: A Guide to the Man and His Music*, ed. Louis Biancolli (New York: Grosset & Dunlap, 1962), p. 179.

Giovanni has few of the social implications of *Figaro*, and the institution of *ius primae noctis* has no central importance in the drama. Masetto may resent Don Giovanni as an interloping nobleman, but neither he nor his neighbors would be hunting him down if Don Giovanni were a feudal lord asserting traditional prerogatives. Certainly, Zerlina never thinks of him in this way. She is just a milkmaid who fancies for a moment that she can marry above her station. Why bother with Masetto if you can have a Don as a husband?

But even this eagerness to climb the social ladder is secondary in Zerlina's character. Of greater significance is the fact that her lowly condition in society enables Zerlina to represent Nature, as opposed to the courtly conventions to which Donna Anna belongs. Zerlina's opening music is utterly and archetypically rural. She and Masetto and the peasants cluck their "la, la, la, la, la, la's" as if they were barnyard fowl. Obviously, they are birds of the same feather as Papageno and Papagena in *The Magic Flute*. Being a product of natural animality, Zerlina advises all the other country lasses to follow her in making hay while the sun shines. And that, of course, is precisely the attitude of Don Giovanni, who observes the spectacle with pleasure. "Che bella gioventù," he says, as if to remind us of Lorenzo de' Medici's poem about fleeting youth:

> Quant'è bella giovinezza,
> Che si fugge tuttavia!
> Chi vuol esser lieto, sia:
> Di doman non c'è certezza.[30]

> [How beautiful is youth,
> Though fleeing evermore.
> Let him who will, be happy!
> Tomorrow nothing's sure.]

In posing as the protector of these young creatures, Don Giovanni—whose very name signifies youth—assumes his natural role as a local Silenus. Zerlina recognizes this immediately, and she gravitates towards him with instincts much deeper than any rites of defloration or rights of the first night. On the contrary, it is merely social restraint (embodied in Masetto and Elvira) that keeps her from instantly uniting with her patron god. Her sensuous

---

[30]Song from *Bacco ed Arianna*. See Luigi Tonelli, *L'Amore nella poesia e nel pensiero del Rinascimento* (Florence: Sansoni, 1933), p. 30.

vacillation—*vorrei, e non vorrei*—is the female counterpart to his glittering technique. The male must always *think* he is leading, that he is forcing the issue, that he is dragging the quivering female into the dream house of sexual delight. He will then feel dominant and may even take responsibility for the outcome. Zerlina follows Don Giovanni in this dance, as she later follows him in the ballroom, and into an adjoining chamber. She protests her weakness in order to elicit support from the assertive male, and in fact she gets promises of love and a glamorous marriage. By the end of their exchange, Zerlina is thoroughly seduced. The voices intertwine melodiously, and she may just as well be added to Don Giovanni's list.[31] She joins him in singing over and over again: "Let us go, let us go, my dear, to relieve the pangs of an innocent love!" What *naturally* follows cannot be shown on the stage, and anyhow only a prude would think of asking, Does she or doesn't she? do they or don't they? It is quite suitable for Elvira to intervene at this point. Her appearance provides the kind of frustration that keeps Don Giovanni going, but also he has symbolically fructified Zerlina, and it little matters that she will bear fruit to someone else.

It is mainly in relation to Masetto that we see how greatly Zerlina approximates Don Giovanni. To achieve her feminine freedoms, she must pretend that the dull and cloddish Masetto is really quite masterful. Though she rejects his complaints against her, she knows she will never convince him of her innocence. In any event, Zerlina has no conception of what it is to be guilty in sexual matters. She only knows what feels good at the moment, and she cannot believe that anything as pleasant as sex could possibly be wrong. She therefore adjusts her appearances to what she thinks Masetto expects of her. And that involves a quasi-masochistic game in which she gets what she wants by making him feel dominant. Since he likes to think she is guilty, let him punish her. She knows it won't hurt; and when it is over, she can expect him to indulge her even further. But this too must all happen off stage. Here she need only sing: "O handsome Masetto, beat, beat your poor Zerlina: I'll stand here like a little lamb and wait for your blows." She is merely

---

[31]On this see Edward T. Cone, *The Composer's Voice* (Berkeley: University of California Press, 1974), p. 155, where Zerlina's "subconscious reaction" to Don Giovanni is shown to reveal itself in the fact that "she appropriates his music, remaking it in accordance with her own style." For musical evidence about Zerlina's possible seduction in the ballroom scene at the end of Act I, see Moberly, *Three Mozart Operas*, pp. 194–95.

seducing him, and even Masetto knows it: "Just see how that witch was able to win me over! [Literally, "seduce me"—*sedurmi.*] Ah, but we men are a weak-headed lot!" If only he could, he would do better to live without her. But they both know that he cannot.

In the opera Masetto does not beat Zerlina, but Don Giovanni beats *him.* When that happens, Zerlina blames it all on Masetto's jealousy. Since he is too miserable to contest this astounding interpretation, she takes his silence as proof of her victory and goes on to heal him by means of her magical sensuousness. If he promises to trust her in the future, she will take him home and apply a panacea that cures all men. It is a fine medicine; it is natural; it does not turn the stomach; the apothecary cannot make it: "It's a certain balm that I carry with me; I can give it to you if you want to try it." Indeed he does! He was created with that in mind. As a final proof of her vital goodness, her *buon natural,* Zerlina makes Masetto feel the beating of her heart. We know that this is not where she carries her medicinal balm, but the heart has always symbolized the sexual regions of the body, and there is no need for her to be more explicit. Moreover, the beating of the heart parallels the beating that she solicited from Masetto earlier; the verb *battere* is used in both places. It also suggests the strokes of sexual intercourse. All three senses of the word reveal the subtle duplicity of her technique: to satisfy her wants by apparently wanting nothing, to seduce the male into seducing her, to give herself as a way of getting him. She thereby cures a "distress" which is not uniquely masculine but which she treats as a consequence of the male need to dominate.

In Ovid, Zerlinas populate the countryside. As with Mozart and Da Ponte, they are always seen from the man's point of view. Ovid thinks of love as a disease that generates its own cure. He illustrates this by an image of Cupid holding in one hand an arrow that libidinally wounds and in the other a box of medicine—as one might expect from the sexual theme, unguent or lubricating jelly. Cupid cures the evil he also inflicts, just as Zerlina does.[32] What the ancient world entrusted to a boyish god, as did the poetry and the iconographic painting of the Renaissance, Mozart and Da Ponte elicit from the sheer femininity of a young woman in nature. In

[32]For further discussion of Ovid's image of Cupid as a literary trope, see my article "Erotic Transformations in the Legend of Dido and Aeneas," *MLN*, December 1975.

Figaro, as we shall see, it is Cherubino, a pubescent Don Giovanni, who bears the Ovidian imagery—or rather, he shares it with the sisterly equivalents of Zerlina. They are all erotic in the same way.

10. The Madness of Elvira

If Zerlina and Donna Anna are abstractions, one belonging to the Don Giovanni principle and the other to the Commendatore's, Donna Elvira is nevertheless a person. The two principles combine in her as they do in Leporello. Perhaps that is why she and Leporello are paired off through much of the action. At the beginning, Don Giovanni puts them together so that Leporello may crudely inform Elvira what the predatory male is like; and then, as if to illustrate the lecture, he arranges for Leporello to act like a Don Juan and run off with Elvira himself. The outcome is no happier for Elvira than for Leporello. But at least it cures her of a hopeless passion. In the final scene with Don Giovanni, she shows that she has learned her lesson; and after his death, she returns to the convent she should never have left in the first place.

For in being divided between the two principles, Elvira cannot survive in the real world. Leporello can: like most normal people, he knows how to temporize between freedom and restraint, between life and death. But Elvira is not normal. She needs the asylum of a protective institution. If marriage cannot provide it, a convent or a mental hospital must. Her division is much deeper than the split between hatred and love for the same man, or even the fact that she wants something she can never have. Don Giovanni and Leporello both say at various times that Donna Elvira is mad. Leporello says it with sympathy, since he is a fellow human being with similar problems; Don Giovanni says it with cynicism and a kind of clinical detachment.

I think we should take these cues at their face value. There is something in the way Elvira loves Don Giovanni, and something in the way she hates him, which is pathological throughout. If this were simply *opera buffa,* the conflict within such a character would make her farcical and nothing else. Since she and her music are always serious, however, her condition is more troublesome than funny. And what a terrible thing it is to see a woman suffer for love as she does and then to become accessories to the pain by laughing, as we must, at her incredible naïveté. *Dramma giocoso* can be a cruel art indeed, suitable to the Spanish setting. Don Quixote and Donna

Elvira—how similar in the pathos of their impossible idealism and in the comedy of their unrelenting madness!

In saying that Elvira's music is always serious, I am referring to the vocal line. The orchestral accompaniment often makes wry or amused comments. But everything she *sings* is earnest in the extreme. In her first aria (*Ah, chi mi dice mai*), the coloratura leaps are so exaggerated as to prepare us for any outlandish behavior on the part of this escaped nun—as she is in Molière. Kierkegaard sees the aria as a complex presentation of love's hatred. He describes it in these words: "Her inmost being is stirred by turbulent emotions, she has aired her grief, she grows faint for a moment, as every passionate outbreak enervates her; there follows a pause in the music. But the turbulence in her inmost being shows clearly that her passion has not reached its full expression; the diaphragm of wrath must yet vibrate more intensely.... Now passion blazes stronger, rages more violently within her, and bursts forth in sound. Once again it repeats itself; then her emotion shakes her to the depths of her soul, and wrath and pain pour forth like a stream of lava in the celebrated run with which the aria ends."[33]

As Kierkegaard's description suggests, Elvira's aria is love finding its only consummation in a hate-filled parody of itself. And as hatred parodies the love in Elvira, the scene itself mocks the personal character of her suffering by letting Don Giovanni and Leporello overhear it all, like peeping toms spying on a lady's privacy. They too are divided with respect to the emotional discharge. Not knowing who she is, Don Giovanni mutters: "Poor little thing! Poor little thing! ... Let's try to console her sorrow." In saying this, he may even be sincere. His expression of concern need not be taken as the wolf licking its chops. But Leporello ridicules the idea of sympathy in Don Giovanni: "That's how he's consoled eighteen hundred of them."

This scene occurs towards the beginning of the opera; and Mozart uses it to prepare us for the conflict between the sensuous and the passionate that will pervade the entire work. The violence of Elvira's aria is continually interrupted by the sensuous music in which Don Giovanni and Leporello make comments about this unknown female. Her agitation in the aria is not incited by Don Giovanni's "jeering laughter," as Kierkegaard says, but rather by the contrasting presence of mere sensuousness. Mozart will not let us focus exclusively upon Elvira's passionate feelings. To make sure

[33]Kierkegaard, *Either/Or*, pp. 120-21.

that we do not sympathize unduly, he further undermines the presentation of her passion by introducing sarcastic thunderbolts hurled from the orchestra. Her vocal line is authentically passionate, but the aria as a whole is ironic and even distorted.

Elvira's division or ambivalence never leaves her. Even at the end, her inner conflict cannot resolve itself. In her final scene, her love for Don Giovanni develops as far as it can go, but it is not strong enough to fight the negative spirit of the Commendatore. As Don Giovanni had offered to console her in the first act, she now tries to save his soul. Don Giovanni distrusts her motivation, and he is right. It is hard to know what she really wants. We can recognize her gesture as the effort of a loving woman; even Leporello takes it that way. But when Don Giovanni refuses to change his life, she turns on him with all the viciousness that characterized her first entrance. She still wants her revenge.

At this point, Leporello comments on Don Giovanni's "heart of stone," which prepares us for the business of the Statue. When the Commendatore avenges himself, he also avenges that much of Elvira that will never cease to hate Don Giovanni. In the later Romantic versions of the myth, Don Juan can be saved only by a woman's perfect devotion. And it comes to him with remarkable frequency. If Donna Elvira cannot save Don Giovanni, perhaps it is because Mozart and Da Ponte did not believe in the purity of her passion. Nor would it have met the elevated standards of the following century.

Between the first and last scenes, Elvira oscillates wildly between the two principles in her nature. She is always in torment, as if they cannot really be reconciled. Just as Anna wants vengeance for her father's death and begins to calm herself when that seems imminent, Donna Elvira is out to "avenge my deceived heart." But this cannot be done while the heart is still palpitating. It must first stop or chill itself, as in any number of Renaissance tragedies. If it still beats with the passionate hope that Elvira retains until the end, it *may* cause injury to the false beloved but it will certainly visit the greatest revenge upon itself. Mozart understood this very well, and his music portrays the pathology of passion with the accuracy of a great physician. Elvira does not perceive what is going on because she knows so little about herself and about the world. Leporello says she speaks like "a printed book"—i.e., a fanciful romance—and so he whips out his own little book of names in order to put her in touch with reality. This merely infuriates her. After the catalogue scene, she is beside herself with rage and threatens to do something desperate. But what are we to think of her as Leporello sings about his master's artfulness? She does not leave. She listens.

Da Ponte is often criticized for having Elvira remain there in silence and take it all. Occasionally, a kindly stage director will give her a bench to sit on while ruminating on her ruin. But generally she just stands around, glancing at the list perhaps, and doubtless memorizing every word. I myself think of her awkward position in this scene as yet another sign of her unworldliness. Throughout the length of Leporello's insulting aria, she is hypnotized by the mere fact of masculine deceit. She stays silent because she is dumbfounded and aghast. She had *no idea* that the world could be such a place, just as she never learns that screaming at a faithless husband is not the best way of getting him to return. When Leporello ends with the remark "voi sapete quel che fa," he touches the most sensitive nerve of all. For in her uncontrollable torment and schizophrenic isolation, she does *not* know much about the doings of Don Giovanni or what he has done to her. She gnashes her teeth and goes off to avenge her suffering heart; but all she knows is how to make it suffer more.

Elvira's idea of revenge appears shortly afterwards, when she sees Don Giovanni flirting with Zerlina. Revenge consists in preventing him from doing with others what he has already done with her. Ostensibly, this is a moral act that saves innocent girls from committing the same mistake that she has made. But also it keeps her in contact with the brute and frightens off all competition. When Don Giovanni tells Zerlina that the poor thing carries on like this because she is madly in love with him, he is not falsifying the situation.

Because Elvira's madness is still love after all, she is more than eager to accept Don Giovanni's protestations in the balcony scene. Like her own servant girl, she cannot resist the pleading of a man who says: "Ah, believe me! or I'll kill myself!" She desperately *wants* to believe him. When she vacillates and says, "I don't know whether to go or to stay," she duplicates the "vorrei e non vorrei" of Zerlina, and perhaps of all women in love. But from the very start we knew that the matter was hopeless, not only because Don Giovanni has let us in on his plans, but also because Elvira has just been telling that unreasonable heart of hers not to pity this man. And so we intuit that with that ruthlessness, measure for measure, which runs throughout the opera, Don Giovanni will have no pity on *her*. He will deceive her to the top of his erotic bent; and at the most pathetic moment of her vacillation, when even Leporello begs the gods to

protect her trusting soul, he will pride himself on the sheer versatility of his talent.

Though Elvira tells her heart to have no pity, she herself can
never accept the idea of measure for measure. Agreeing to renounce Don Giovanni in the final scene—which is, after all, the one
thing he now wants of her—she offers him that *pietà* which Donna
Anna hoped to get from heaven some day. But the transition to this
emotional alternative must have seemed too abrupt to Mozart. At
the Vienna premiere he added the recitative and aria that begin
with the phrase "In quali eccessi." Here we see the conflict in Elvira's soul more sharply articulated than anywhere else: vengefulness
against love, hatred against pity. Love and pity win out, but the
suffering is terrible.

In itself, but above all, as compared to *Ah, chi mi dice mai,* this
aria is profoundly moving. It is powerful in its vehemence but also
deeply sympathetic towards a woman who can still love a man like
that, limited and imperfect as her love may be. Taken all in all,
Mozart's Elvira has the complexity of a real person. Her conflict
cannot be resolved, and nothing will enable her to live in the world;
but at least she is beginning to understand her disability. From
having been ridiculous, pathetic, silly, and mad, she now emerges
as a tragic heroine. She almost, though not quite, turns into Dido
lamenting the loss of love—a favorite theme for eighteenth-century
opera. Unlike Dido, she does not kill herself now that she knows
her lover will not return. Instead her conflict remains forever
fixed, diminishing perhaps through attrition or inner friction, but
in the no exit of passional hell continuing as a permanent equilib-
rium which is her death-in-life. Don Giovanni descends into the
nether regions, where he will find new adventures, like Dante on
his way to Beatrice. But Elvira buries herself in the convent. She
merely sits there, in an overheated cubicle reserved for women who
have learned something from loving a Don Juan, though not
enough to cure themselves.

11. The Division in Mozart

Thus even in damnation, and by contrast to those who are
spared, Don Giovanni retains an indestructible vitality. Though
everyone stands against him, he is the only character who enjoys
the entire experience. He is the embodiment of everyone's sensuous inclinations. The opera idealizes them, expresses them as vivid

and compelling possibilities. Even in punishing Don Giovanni as a libertine, the work scarcely affirms a contrary way of life. It merely condemns him for being passionate about the sensuous. Passion is bad, Mozart seems to say, in Don Giovanni as well as Elvira. In her, it leads to madness; in him, to heartless cruelty. But in Don Giovanni, passion is always directed towards something Mozart values very highly: freedom to express one's natural playfulness, to take one's pleasure as one wishes, to sport with sounds and words and deeds and people, and in general to enjoy the sensuous aggressiveness of an emancipated male. As Rolland says, Mozart puts himself into Don Giovanni: "If one studies Don Juan a little closer, one sees in his brilliance, his selfishness, his teasing spirit, his pride, his sensuality, and his anger, the very traits that may be found in Mozart himself."[34]

Still, Rolland is wrong to neglect the differences between Mozart and Don Giovanni. They are not the same. Don Giovanni is not really human. Nor is Mozart limited to an abstract principle. He loved the sensuous, but he feared its total liberation. Though Don Giovanni is his hero, he also sides with the forces that destroy him. The good life, as Mozart saw it, would not turn sensuousness into a passion or make a religion of it. The sensuous is holy, but the Knight of Sensuousness must be annihilated.

12. The Conflict Both Resolved and Unresolved

Don Giovanni is not the only Mozart opera that pits the sensuous against the passionate. But unlike the others, it creates dramatic tensions that it cannot resolve completely. The Statue takes Don Giovanni to hell, and the Epilogue assures us that now everything will work itself out for the best. But we have been so captivated by the vitality of our musical monster that we cannot easily imagine the world without him. Being divided between love and fear of what is merely sensuous, Mozart will neither change the traditional ending nor treat it with the doctrinal respect it once commanded. With one hand he gives the Statue awesome chords and those ominous trombones; with the other, he makes it difficult for us to see any serious dogma in this. Assaulted in the final scene by the wind-machine, the banging timpani, the eery voices of devils underground, we can only cower like Leporello under the table.

[34]Rolland, *Essays on Music,* p. 257.

The music is fearful, frightening in its melodramatic effect; but we also know that Don Giovanni is right to scorn the pretentiousness of it all, to oppose the noisy spectacle, to reject it as mere appearance and clamorous unreality. The result has often been a disruption of audience response, a puzzlement that is not easily removed.

This peculiarity of *Don Giovanni* has been recognized by many critics. In the twentieth century, they tend to separate into two camps. At one extreme are those who consider the opera essentially chaotic, artistically unformed, and even unfinished. At the other extreme are those who find an existential paradox within the ontology that Mozart expresses.

One might think that Kierkegaard would represent the existentialist interpretation; but actually he disqualifies himself by refusing to see any religious significance in the work, treating it as merely the exposition of sensuousness and the immediately aesthetic. More recent writers have sought to emphasize theological as well as aesthetic elements that combine to make the opera distinctly existentialist. For instance, Geoffrey Clive insists upon a coexistence or mutual interplay of joy and nothingness: "The central theme in *Don Giovanni* is the intermingling of freedom and dread. ... No discursive mediation of these two elements is possible, yet Mozart's music, without destroying the authenticity of either, expresses joyful affirmation always on the edge of profound nihilism."[35]

As against the existentialist position, Joseph Kerman says:

> Kierkegaard first spoke of a magic "marriage" between the genius of Mozart and the subject matter of Don Juan, and many have followed him in this view. I could not disagree more completely.... As an opera composer, Mozart had dwelt more profoundly than anyone else on man in relation to other men and women, never in relation to God and the universe. Then suddenly theology was thrust on him at the end of *Don Giovanni*—right at the end, when things were getting rushed, as usual. He did his best, a very wonderful best, but everything we know or feel about Mozart should assure us that the inflexible view of sin and death set forth in the legend must have been distasteful to him. Mozart never saw man's will as inevitably opposed by the will of God. He conceived an essential harmony expressed by human feelings; his terms were brotherhood and sympathy and

[35]Geoffrey Clive, *The Romantic Enlightenment* (New York: Meridian Books, 1960), pp. 44, 55.

humility, not damnation and defiance. The magic marriage is
The Magic Flute.[36]

Earlier Kerman had remarked that instead of ending in "honest
and subtle equivocation," the opera degenerates into "accidental
and unformed ambiguity." His criticism resembles T. S. Eliot's
claim that *Hamlet* is a "failure" because in it Shakespeare grapples
with "an emotion which he cannot express in art."[37] Unfortunately,
Kerman's argument is weakened by at least two flaws in his reasoning. First, he begs the question when he asserts that the Don Juan
legend sets forth an "inflexible view of sin and death." Nothing
could be more flexible than the sources in Molière and the Com-
media dell'Arte from which Da Ponte drew his text; and even Tirso's version of the myth reopens and reexamines the Catholic view
of sin and death rather than presenting it inflexibly. Second, Kerman distorts the existentialist argument. It does not characterize
Mozart's theological pole as being conventional in its dogma, but
only a recognition that man lives in dread and that death signifies
the nothingness of his being. Without being an ultramontanist or
even an orthodox believer, Mozart could very well have used the
final scenes to express this kind of attitude.

It seems to me that the existentialist position is overdone, however, and that Kerman is right in emphasizing *The Magic Flute* as
the doctrinal opera among Mozart's works. *Don Giovanni* is not
unformed or aesthetically accidental in its ambiguity, but neither
does it provide an ideological resolution. It states a problem—the
problem of the virile male whose natural instincts are defeated not
only by social restraints and Christian morality, but also by a conflict between the sensuous and the passionate within human nature. In merely presenting the problem, working at it but reaching
no final conclusions, *Don Giovanni* is the most analytical of the
Mozart operas. The work is not existentialist, since it nowhere affirms the paradox of being and nothingness. To do so, it would
have had to present each with equal importance, and it certainly
does not do that. For all the doom and damnation of the final
scene, the opera concerns itself mainly with the vicissitudes of the
life force. In this sense, and despite its denouement, it is basically

[36]Kerman, *Opera as Drama*, pp. 122–23. On Mozart's problems with composing,
see Erich Hertzmann, "Mozart's Creative Process," in *The Creative World of Mozart*,
ed. Paul Henry Lang (New York: W. W. Norton, 1963).
[37]T. S. Eliot, "Hamlet and His Problems," in *Selected Essays* (New York: Harcourt, Brace, 1950), p. 126.

naturalistic. The wild and daemonic quest for freedom may have troubled Mozart as a threat to the moral order in society, and perhaps that explains the fearful ending of the opera. But death and retribution, hellfire and the unbending Statue, would still function as mere impediments within the search for life. They interfere with the progress of the sensuous male, and may even end it for reasons of morality, but they have no autonomous being of their own. They do not represent nothingness or dread as an ontological category.

The spirit of Don Giovanni pervades this opera so thoroughly that it even gives life to the Statue. Though he provides the Commendatore with his own musical themes, Mozart infuses them with the swirling movement that expresses Don Giovanni's passionate dedication to the sensuous. The overture is constructed out of the dramatic intermingling of music for the two characters. They sing together in the first and final scenes as participants in the same world of vital plenitude, a world in which desires crave fulfillment and instincts seek their natural goal—whether in sex or parental protectiveness. In *The Magic Flute* Mozart appeals to Reason as the means of controlling and purifying this world; but even then he shows no inclination to go beyond it through a sense of nothingness.

To see this, we need only compare *Don Giovanni* (or *The Magic Flute,* for that matter) with the Requiem Mozart thought he was writing for himself and which he did not finish. The Requiem may be called "accidental and unformed," inasmuch as it tries to express traditional dogmas that Mozart could no longer accept. As Dent puts it: "The words of the Requiem insist constantly upon just that fear of death which Freemasonry has taught Mozart to overcome."[38] As a result, the music fails to express either the sublimity or the dread of an authentic religious attitude. The Requiem has little of *The Magic Flute*'s cosmic amplitude—that sense of an infinite progression for the spirit, in freedom and serenity, through life and into death. Yet neither does the Requiem express the feeling of nothingness with the profundity that characterizes so much of Mozart's music in this period. One can only conclude that existential insight was not a part of his particular genius.

Perhaps that is why Mozart allowed Da Ponte to follow Molière in one surprising but very crucial detail of the final scene. While Don Giovanni remains constant in his mission, he is tricked by the

[38]*Mozart's Operas,* pp. 252–53.

other-worldly visitor who claims to partake of celestial food. The Statue asks for Don Giovanni's hand as a pledge that he will dine with him, but then drags Don Giovanni down to hell. In other words, even the principal agent of moral rectitude has been seduced and corrupted by that devious dishonesty for which Don Giovanni must be punished. In this opera, death and destruction do not indicate an ultimate solution. They intrude upon the problems of life, but they scarcely reveal an alternative to them.

Don Giovanni is not a religious tragedy. It is black comedy of a kind that no other musical composition has ever been able to approximate. And so extraordinary is its success as a work of art that it overcomes all ideological difficulties. It does so by fully exploiting the expressive potentialities of music. As Otto Rank points out, discussing Mozart's division in *Don Giovanni*, "The capability of expressing different emotions simultaneously makes music especially well suited to the presentation and affective resolution of ambivalence ... [in the case of this opera, the] tension between unchecked sensuality and the guilt and punishment tendency."[39] I think this approach is correct. In his genius Mozart shows us (as Shakespeare also does) how an artist may often harmonize conflicting emotions in a work of art that expresses their constant warfare magnificently but provides no other solution. The manic sexuality of Don Giovanni merges with the sublime sensuousness of musical sound, the moral inhibitions of the repressive Commendatore survive as the formal constraints that guide artistic creativity, and both perspectives are fused within the great harmony of an aesthetic oneness which transcends antinomies and unifies principles that might otherwise have remained eternally irreconcilable. What cannot be effected through mere rationality, or even lived emotion, is thus accomplished through art alone.

[39]Rank, *The Don Juan Legend*, p. 126.

CHAPTER III

Mozart: *Figaro,*
Così, & *The Magic Flute*

Among the Mozart operas, only *Don Giovanni* uses the conflict between the sensuous and the passionate as a dominant theme. Nevertheless, it enters into the other major works as well: in *The Marriage of Figaro* subordinate to the comedy of intrigue; in *Così fan tutte* submerged within the battle of the sexes, each of which suffers from a similar conflict; and in *The Magic Flute* as part of man's animality that must be transcended through Reason. The three Italian operas written in collaboration with Da Ponte make a unified triptych within themselves. But *The Magic Flute,* like the earlier German singspiel *The Abduction from the Seraglio,* also contributes to a pattern that is very largely woven out of the concepts we have been examining.

I. *Figaro* and the Politics of the Sensuous

In the conversation in the graveyard, Don Giovanni tells Leporello how he has made the most ("approfitto") of the fact that a beautiful young girl took him to be Leporello himself. Horrified, the servant asks, What if she had been my wife? To which Don

74

Giovanni replies that that would have been better yet. The idea for this exchange must have come to Da Ponte from the *Figaro* which he and Mozart had adapted from Beaumarchais's play a year or so earlier. For there the plot concerns itself almost entirely with an aristocrat's attempts to seduce the young girl who is soon to be his servant's wife. Like the maid Don Giovanni serenades, Susanna is also the servant of the seducer's own wife. The Conte Almaviva woos Susanna almost as persuasively as Don Giovanni in his manoeuvers with Zerlina; and the music of the *Sì* and *No* duet duplicates in its sensuous ambivalence the erotic modalities of *Vorrei e non vorrei.* As Zerlina is protected by Elvira, so is Susanna by the Countess—who resembles Elvira in being an abandoned and therefore repressive wife. Figaro, who gets slapped several times but eventually finds comfort in the soothing sexuality of Susanna, anticipates Masetto as well as Leporello. He pretends to make love to the Countess, like Leporello sporting with Elvira, and he too represents the sensibility of the ordinary male.

To draw these parallels, however, is not enough. In fact they can be very misleading. For the two operas are really quite dissimilar in many respects. In *Figaro* the question of passion, and its relationship to the sensuous life, is hardly exploited. Despite what Stendhal says about insights into "urgent and heart-felt passions" in *Figaro,* the opera deals mainly with the nature and vicissitudes of sensuousness. *Don Giovanni* consists of a series of episodes in which the sexual hero tests his passionate devotion to the sensuous against a hostile environment. In *Figaro,* however, the drama occurs within the sensuous itself. The work is primarily devoted to the politics of sensuousness as various cliques struggle for power within its domain. Figaro is not outraged by the Count's attitude towards Susanna. He considers it the "most natural" thing in the world. He opposes it because it interferes with his own designs, not because he is passionately angered or even passionately in love with Susanna. When Figaro thinks that she has betrayed him and that he will catch her in the arms of the Count, like Vulcan snaring Venus in the net with Mars, he puts his energy into scheming about steps to be taken rather than feeling anything deeply.

Indeed how can he? He happens to think of Venus because he has been looking into the star-filled night. "Tutto è tranquillo, e placido!" he says; and Mozart fits the mood with pretty music suitable to classical reminiscences but not to heartfelt passion or burning jealousy. Throughout the opera the passionate lies just below the surface, and Figaro tells his mother that Susanna's conduct has hurt him very much; but strong feelings are rarely expressed in the music or developed in the drama.

The overture itself is purely sensuous. It is Mozart at his sky-blue best, with none of those frightening adumbrations that give the overture to *Don Giovanni* its dark and troublesome complexion. The opening music to *Figaro* is simply a continuous flow of melody, seamless and single-minded. When the curtain rises, we see Figaro measuring a rococo bedroom, not Leporello pacing nervously while his master is forcing a woman to his will. There is no problem about the delightful experience which the bedroom symbolizes, only about its location between the chambers of the Count and the Countess. And this is important for reasons that are wholly political: the bedroom gives the Count access to Susanna, while separating him from the Countess. To meet the situation, Figaro must use his wits, not his emotions. When he begs Susanna to spare him the details of her fears—"Susanna, pian pian"—we may imagine him contriving to keep the Count from overhearing them rather than trying to protect himself against her frankness. In his cavatina *Se vuol ballare, signor contino,* he and his music dance with the lightness of Don Giovanni's sensuous serenade even though Figaro sings with an intonation of vindictiveness and bitter satisfaction. For he is thinking of the pleasure in outsmarting the Count, in teaching him a lesson about sex, as he once taught him how to steal that very Rosina who has now become the Countess.

There is something sensuous about intrigue itself, for it stimulates the imagination into one artful position after another without allowing passionate involvement to intrude. Figaro schemes against the Count in order to keep Susanna from his clutches; but one feels that what Figaro loves most in life is the scheming itself. In Beaumarchais, Susanna says to Figaro at one point: "Plotting and pocketing—you're in your element."[1] Through its sheer sensuous texture, Mozart's music conveys the idea better than any words could do.

In *Don Giovanni* none of the characters is really likeable. The conflict between the sensuous and the passionate makes each of them seem pathological to varying degrees, or at least tainted by moral ugliness. In *Figaro,* however, all the characters are im-

[1] *Beaumarchais' Figaro's Marriage,* trans. Jacques Barzun (New York: Farrar, Straus & Cudahy, 1961). I use this translation throughout, except for Figaro's diatribe, which I chose to translate myself.

mediately ingratiating—with the exception of the Count. At times he is even offensive. He is too real in his nastiness to be a mere *buffone;* and yet, tricking and defeating him gives us the same pleasure as it does with outright comic figures like Monostatos in *The Magic Flute,* Osmin in *The Abduction,* and any number of other representatives of male sexuality at its predatory worst: Rossini's Bartolo, Wagner's Beckmesser, Strauss's Baron Ochs, etc. Yet the Count differs from these characters in being the unquestioned ruler of the political entity within which the opera occurs. He bears a corresponding nobility and is not simply a fool. He is the legitimate authority. By opposing him with characters who—*in their musical expressiveness*—are as sympathetic as Susanna, Figaro, and the Countess, the opera makes a revolutionary statement different from, but just as radical as, the original version in Beaumarchais.

Napoleon cited Beaumarchais's play as one of the major causes of the French Revolution. In its own way, Mozart's opera may have been equally subversive. In both the play and the opera, the action consists in the democratization of the sensuous. What formerly belonged to the aristocracy—a sporting attitude towards sex—now belongs to everyone. Figaro and Susanna can play the game as well as the Count, though their goal is matrimony rather than promiscuity. But where Beaumarchais attacks the privileges of the old regime through political satire, which caused his work to be banned, Mozart employs a technique that is less easily censored and possibly more effective. He disarms the audience through melodies that linger and make even the most extensive changes in society seem natural or harmonious as possibilities. By giving them beautiful music (and many of the best arias), he makes the little people sound as glamorous as the noblemen of earlier generations. And since he expresses these ideas through music, his political position cannot be refuted or attacked by the discursive intellect. Yet his revolutionary intent persists from beginning to end. By striking at the sexual authority, the male seducer who also runs the state, Mozart's music relentlessly—just think of the continuous pitter-patter of the orchestra in every scene—eats away at the social order, like an ocean endlessly gnawing at the shore.[2]

In previous operas the male head of the household had often been outfoxed by his servants, even in matters of his own sexuality.

---

[2]For a contrary view about *Figaro* as a revolutionary work, cf. Joseph Kerman, "Marriages in *Figaro*," in *The Opera News Book of Figaro,* ed. Frank Merkling (New York: Dodd, Mead, 1967), pp. 43-44. See also Brigid Brophy, "'Figaro' and the Limitations of Music," *Music and Letters,* January 1970.

This happens in Pergolesi's masterpiece *La Serva Padrona,* written some fifty years earlier. But there, Ubaldo is quite likeable, more so than the girl to whom he loses. In any event, his struggle is purely individual. The entire state does not depend upon its outcome. In Mozart the *droit du seigneur,* the privilege of defloration that the Count seeks to exercise, represents all his other rights as well. In their attempts to effect a change in the status quo, the conspirators stand together in a burst of nonviolent political action. As if they all belonged to some preestablished harmony, they communicate with each other (and with the orchestra, which is wholly partisan to their cause) through the subtlest of musical cues. They are like bats that navigate through sonic means alone. We almost feel they can read one another's mind, like those characters in novels by Henry James who finish each other's sentences with an uncanny awareness of the singular world in which they live. Even the Count belongs to this oneness in the sound. He is not to be wholly excluded, emasculated, or divested of power; he is merely to be chastened and reformed, blended into that general will of which Rousseau spoke but only Mozart could articulate in music.

As a result, the Count is always both in and out of the musical community. But, in a sense, this is true of all the other characters too. None of them knows exactly what is going on in any one scene. After defeating the Count in a series of manoeuvers, thanks to the whispered hints of Susanna and the Countess, Figaro hears him say: "It's all a mystery to me." To which Figaro comments in an aside: "The poor fellow knows even less about it all than I do." With their interspersed "Stelle!" and "O, Ciel!" the ladies seem to feel an equal confusion throughout the opera. From moment to moment, and as individuals, the characters are all lost in the sea that washes over them. Yet in it they find a musical being that links them each to each, eventually ending in the harmony of a double matrimony plus a marital reconciliation. The revolution has now succeeded; and presumably the world will be more conducive to the liberty, fraternity, and equality of sensuous—though not promiscuous—love.

Although he represents male dominance and the need to assert it through seduction, the Count has none of Don Giovanni's sense of freedom. He is a worried seducer, not a frivolous one. Where Don Giovanni charms the ladies by offering a refuge from convention, the Count must always think of his position as a husband and head of state. When he was younger—in *The Barber of Seville,* for instance—he too ran about in disguise captivating women with his gaiety and daring. But now, he and his authoritarian roles are inseparable. His lovemaking is therefore ridden with reverberations of guilt that never issue from a Don Giovanni who has no authority and knows that those who do are out to destroy him.

Furthermore, Don Giovanni realizes that the game of seduction depends upon freedom in both participants. If the woman succumbs to institutional force, the act proves nothing about one's sexual prowess. Don Giovanni wishes to seduce females as a way of establishing his excellence as a male, and therefore he does not rely upon political power. That line from Stendhal is worth quoting again, for it applies more precisely to the Count than to Don Giovanni: "*Power* is only the greatest happiness, after love, because one imagines that one is in a position to *command sympathy.*"

The Count may ultimately have the same goals as Don Giovanni, but he is always thwarted by that public mask he loves so well and will not remove under any circumstances. He knows it dazzles women, and he fears they will not yield to him without it. But seeing the world through the barrier it imposes, he constantly confuses personal charm with his privileged condition, thereby rendering himself ridiculous. Don Giovanni fools others in an attempt to liberate himself. He fails, but he is not ridiculous. The Count fools only himself, which is why his subordinates can frustrate his desires so easily. In the attempt to combine sex and power, love and authority, sympathy and dominance, his affairs lead to ever-increasing humiliation. Only fidelity to the Countess can show him the way out of the fly-bottle. But that solution hardly enters into the opera, even though it is prominent in the play. In Beaumarchais the Count asks Figaro about difficulties with his wife: "What motive did the Countess have for playing that trick on me? . . . I anticipate all her wishes and smother her with gifts." To which Figaro replies: "You give but you aren't faithful: would anyone be grateful for luxuries who is starved of necessities?" In Da Ponte's libretto these lines do not appear; and it is only in the music of reconciliation between Figaro and Susanna at the end of the last act that Mozart expresses the idea of marital fidelity.

It is often remarked that Don Giovanni has few arias even though his musical presence holds the opera together as if by magnetism. This is not surprising if one thinks of the Don as a principle and not a person. Even the Champagne Aria and the Serenade to Elvira's servant are moments of action rather than introspection, revealing a technique rather than a personality. The Count Almaviva is, however, a person—not just a lively spirit, as his name suggests. Each time he apologizes to the Countess, we feel that something is developing in this man. When he finally yields to her moral superiority, we know that he has grown as a human being, that he has learned a little, and even that the concept of fidelity is beginning to dawn upon him. Don Giovanni does not change, for better or worse. He merely shows himself forth, with a constant boldness that approximates courage and contrasts with his inconstancy in lovemaking. He cherishes mutability and runs after the passing show, but *within* him nothing ever happens.

With the Count something internal is always going on. In the aria *Vedrò, mentr'io sospiro*, we see how negative his inner churning can be, how petty and vicious he is capable of becoming. We are not amused; the spectacle is almost embarrassing. We do not laugh, as we did when Bartolo sang his set piece about revenge. That was strictly comic, and at times Mozart infuses the Count's aria with repetitious emphases and upward jumps that give it a similar absurdity. But now the absurdity is that of a real person, those querulous staccati signifying rage in a man who is regressing to childish petulance. The aria uncovers passions and frustrations which we might have surmised from the pervasive vanity of the Count but which the opera does not reveal as clearly in any other place. Beaumarchais arranges for the Count to keep telling us about the quality of his passions, but Mozart and Da Ponte generally submerge them as elements within the ongoing intrigue. Only in this one aria does the Count really expose himself.

That the Count is a person and not a principle like Don Giovanni is evident from his relationship to Cherubino. He hates him as a rival for Barberina, Susanna, and the Countess, but he also fears him as a symbol of the innocent sensuousness that the Count cannot regain—assuming he ever had it. Cherubino may brashly kiss Susanna on the cheek, but he would never take advantage of her helplessness, as the Count does when she faints in the first act. The Count even feels threatened by the fact that Cherubino enjoys his budding sexuality. The Count himself seems to enjoy very little. We never see in him—as we often do in Don Giovanni—the *ability* to savor those pleasures of love or sexuality to which his actions are dedicated. It is as if he has so weary an appetite that for him the erotic life consists *only* of pursuit and conquest. Cherubino may well upset him. Though his feelings may be superficial, Cherubino really feels something. He does not need to use complicated means of self-arousal. In flitting from one girl to another, he is an adolescent

Don Giovanni who succeeds by his innocence alone. He seduces by being seduced. He cannot command and has no power to impose. He is therefore a girlish youth; and by giving him a soprano voice, Mozart perfectly fulfills Beaumarchais's demand that the role be played by a pretty girl "pour en bien sentir les finesses."

The women of the household humor the Count in his domestic tyranny, but they like Cherubino. They find him attractive and even loveable. They can identify with his weak condition while also mothering him into a more docile manhood than could be expected of a boorish male who keeps shouting, as the Count does, "Io voglio! Io voglio!"—"I want, I want." In his teenage confusion of moods, Cherubino flatters women just by admitting that he does *not* know what he wants of them. He is a prey to emotions he cannot control. He confesses to spells in which he burns and then freezes—the alternate extremes that Don Giovanni experiences as he is dragged down to hell—and he describes a narcissism in himself that makes him seem delicate as a flower, incapable of outward attack. It is interesting that Figaro, who uses the word *Narcisetto* for Cherubino, also refers to the Count as a Narcissus. Certainly they are each self-centered in their attitude towards love. But where Cherubino sees only himself because his interpersonal vision has not yet matured, the Count wilfully rejects a concern for other people. Cherubino needs the experiences of life; the Count needs moral reformation.

Because he has an instinct for flattering women, Cherubino knows that they pride themselves on their wisdom in matters of love. He himself is a mythic continuation of Eros, the boyish (but sometimes effeminate) god of love whom we often see in his baby fat as a winged cherub or sexless *putto*. When he appeals to the ladies in his canzona *Voi che sapete / Che cosa è amor* ("You who know what manner of thing love is"), he is asking them for information about himself. The canzona is accompanied by a pizzicato in the strings which gives a tripping effect quite suitable for a mobile young man who has already told us that every woman makes his heart flutter. The accompaniment also adumbrates Don Giovanni's mandoline as he serenades Elvira's maid. And like the Don's serenade, Cherubino's canzona draws upon the troubadours for its inspiration. It has been compared to Dante's *Donne ch'avete intelletto d'amore,* but to me it sounds more like Provençal poetry; and in concluding that Cherubino actually *likes* the torments of love, it reminds us of Chrétien de Troyes saying that of all the evils in life "le mien diffère; il me plaît."

But though these hints of masochistic suffering might suggest deep-rooted passions, Cherubino's canzona gives us no reason to believe that he feels any strong emotion. In its light and lilting melody, with the strings plucking gaily underneath, the song is almost a parody of troubadour longing. In the earlier aria *Non so più cosa son, cosa faccio,* the voice moves too quickly and traverses too many short syllables for us to take it seriously. Moreover, it is supported by an especially "sensuous tone of the clarinet," as Edward Downes remarks.[3] Though Cherubino gets excited by the mere mention of love and spends his time talking about it to the flowers, the trees, the fountains, the echoes (once again, identifying him with Narcissus), we can only see him as a child playing sensuously with his own feelings rather than as a passionate lover yearning for some unattainable beloved. It is worth mentioning that in Beaumarchais Cherubino sings only a popular ballad based on folk poetry. The ballad expresses a picaresque interest in searching for one's sweetheart; and it is sung to the soldierly tune of Malbrouck, which adds to its hearty and martial character. In his usual way, Mozart does something very different. To words of Da Ponte that *could* have been made fervent, he writes sensuous music that precludes any possibility of passion.

In manifesting this innocent play between the sensuous and the passionate, Cherubino inevitably appears to the Count as something less than virile. Though he is not present at the scene in which Susanna and the Countess transform Cherubino into a fetching maiden, playing with his gender as if he were a doll, the Count gets the point just as well. Whether Cherubino is a rival or a sissy or just a traitor to male dominance, he must be banished. The Count cannot tolerate anything that subverts masculine authority, which he defines as his own type of sexuality. Cherubino must therefore be sent into the army. This will get him out of the way for the time being; but also it will make him into the kind of man the Count himself has become. So he thinks and so does Figaro—whose vigorous disposition cannot comprehend an amorous butterfly like Cherubino. They are both mistaken. Love always finds a way. Cherubino sneaks back disguised as a peasant girl, and later flirts with the Countess in his usual puerile manner. The Count's influence fails with him as it does with everyone else. As they had got Cherubino to kneel, while dressing him, the women bring the

[3]Edward Downes, "A Tender Irony," in Merkling, ed., *Figaro,* p. 10.

Count to his knees as well. "Voi che sapete" reminds us of the words that Leporello used with Elvira to indicate her complicity in Don Giovanni's powers of seduction. Here it is the women who know so much about love that they finally manoeuver the men out of their customary aggressiveness and into a tame domesticity that even the wily Figaro may have difficulty escaping.

At the same time, I wonder whether these women do know what love is. Though they occasionally speak of longing, suffering, jealousy, they seem to have only the slightest experience of passion. In *Porgi amor* the Countess introduces herself as a self-pitying woman who laments instead of demanding. Her languorous aria gives one a sense of yielding rather than yearning, of great capacity for patience but few strong desires of her own. In Beaumarchais the Count complains about wives, such as his own, who "are so compliant and constant, always and without stint, that suddenly one day one finds satiety where one looked for happiness." No one *says* anything like this in Mozart's opera, but his music for the Countess continually suggests that she has now become that kind of wife. Though she is worthy of love, the Countess (as Mozart portrays her) is not a very exciting woman. How can one expect her to satisfy the restless appetite of an Almaviva? The Count gravitates towards Susanna not only because she is forbidden fruit, and because he wishes to outdo Figaro, but also because she is vivacious beyond anything the Countess could easily imagine.

In several places, Beaumarchais had given the Countess biting lines to indicate her strength of character. But in the arias that Mozart wrote for her, she sings with a satin loveliness that makes her appear dreamy and somewhat absent to current realities. She keeps returning to the past, as in *Dove sono i bei momenti,* never realizing that she can keep her husband's interest only by exciting him in the present and the future. Susanna lives for the moment, and she welcomes the advent of new sexual pleasures, as in *Deh vieni, non tardar, o gioia bella,* with a freshness of melody that would stimulate any adventuresome male. In giving them such different music, Mozart is emphasizing the fact that Susanna looks forward to matrimony whereas the Countess has already been married several years to a difficult husband. But even so, one cannot believe that Figaro will feel the need to search for extramarital pleasures in the way that anyone married to Mozart's Countess would. For all her warmth and sensibility, she seems too gentle for sex—whether sensuous or passionate. Only Cherubino really desires her, and his is the love of a child for its melancholy mother. He would like to console her. He knows she needs, and possibly wants, that most of all.

For her part, Susanna seems too certain of her sexual allure to feel any great passion. In the *Deh vieni* aria, Mozart conveys her sense of the absolute sweetness which the *piaceri d'amor* will soon provide. They are to her as natural as the sensuous symbols to which she refers—the brook that murmurs, the breeze that whispers and refreshes, the smiling flowers, the glistening grass. Her repeated "Vieni, vieni" awakens desire but not through anything as violent as passion. Her capacity for quick and immediate enjoyment makes that unnecessary. Thwarted, she is either malicious and cutting, as in her duet with Marcellina; or circuitous, as in her clever responses to the Count; or just impulsive, as when she slaps Figaro. The first time that happens, Da Ponte has the onlookers say: "È un effetto di buon core! / Tutto amore è quel che fa!" ("This shows a good heart! It's being in love that makes her do it!"). Mozart presents these words in hushed and reassuring tones, as if the voices were really impressed by the strength of Susanna's emotion. And indeed, her slaps are the strongest and most intimate gestures that love manifests in this opera. They come as a bit of seasoning to sharpen sensuous appetites. They are like the mosquito bite that Proust mentions as a welcome reminder of last summer's vacation. They are a hint (but only a hint) of Susanna's potential depth, of passions that Mozart will depict in Elvira but not in her.

In saying this, however, we must remember that Elvira fails as a woman and as a human being. Susanna and the Countess succeed in both respects, and they do so by resorting to wit and sensuous duplicity rather than passion. It never occurs to Susanna to feel outraged by the indignity of the Count's attentions; nor does the Countess experience anything like Elvira's hatefulness towards Don Giovanni. In the aria *Dove sono*, the Countess vents a disillusionment quite similar to Elvira's, and then attests to the permanence of her love much as Elvira finally does. But though these sentiments are similar, Elvira and the Countess are not. The Countess bears up under the sexual strain. In her marmoreal stolidity, she presents a proud façade. She does not crumble like Elvira, and neither does she allow herself the vengeance she has possibly earned as much as Elvira. She remains constant, and through her constancy she gets her man to return instead of driving him to perdition.

The Countess triumphs through her extraordinary gentleness, the very trait that makes her sexually so disappointing. In the second act she prides herself on being "dolce di core," and then she manages to put the Count into a position where she can show her superiority in being gentler than he. After Figaro and Susanna beg in vain for the Count's forgiveness, she effects the final reconciliation by appearing and forgiving *him.* Kerman uses this brief exchange between the Count and the Countess to prove his thesis that "in opera, the dramatist is the composer." For in Beaumarchais the reconciliation itself amounts to very little. The words that Da Ponte put into the libretto are merely the following:

COUNT:	Contessa perdono!	Forgive me, Countess!
COUNTESS:	Più docile io sono,	I am more gentle
	e dico di sì.	And so I say "yes."
ALL:	Ah tutti contenti	Ah, this way
	saremo così.	We shall all be happy.

As Kerman says, "With this miserable material before him, Mozart built a revelation."[4] Stendhal too had remarked that "Mozart concludes his *Folle Journée* with the most beautiful piece of church-music that can be heard anywhere: the passage occurs after the word: *Perdono!* in the Finale of the whole opera."[5]

The reconciliation that Mozart provides in this music is not only magnificent in its groundswell of expansive harmony but also a serene and fitting culmination to all the petty bickering that has now been put aside. As the composer, he certainly does show himself to be a great dramatist. But while Kerman is right in what he says, he neglects the literary components in Mozart's imagination. *Could* his music have expressed the grandeur of this marital reconciliation without the erotic concepts that led up to it in the opera? I do not think so. Harmony can be established only after the Count is defeated in his wilfulness, but this must occur in a way that does not undermine his masculine authority. Though her motivation was innocent, whereas his was not, the Countess has connived against him with other women and lesser males. At the height of her victory she must therefore affirm even greater submissiveness than in the past. She must give this, rather than leniency towards the guilty, as the basis of her forgiveness: I am more gentle and so I say "yes." Mozart allows no other political arrangement.

---

[4] Kerman, *Opera as Drama,* p. 108.
[5] Stendhal, *Haydn, Mozart, and Metastasio,* p. 202.

Getting the woman to say "yes" has been the Count's problem all along. And with Susanna he could never be sure whether she meant yes or no, regardless of what she said. But here in the finale, the supreme female makes the compliant affirmation for which every male yearns, and she does so at the very moment when she could have been vengeful and destructive. It is because they realize what has been accomplished that the Chorus can sing so joyously. Mozart is indeed the dramatist; but without the expressive concepts that change abstract sounds into concrete significance, we could never have known what either the music or the drama was about.

As the distillation of an ideal enjoyment, Mozart's music is itself the happy resolution the finale promises. For Mozart is interested in more than just saving the Countess's marriage, or even liberating Figaro and Susanna from the sexual domination of the Count. In a moment of transcendence within the complicated intrigues of the second act, he anticipates the ultimate culmination. Here too he takes a few unimpressive words and infuses them with the holy spirit that pervades the entire work. Figaro has just asked the Count to go ahead with the wedding ceremony. The Count is delaying in the hope that Marcellina's lawsuit will make it impossible, but Susanna, Figaro, and the Countess—the three principals in the opera other than the Count himself—beg him in a mellifluent legato to satisfy the lovers' desire:

Susanna	⎱ Deh, Signor	Ah Sir, do not
Figaro	⎰ nol contrastate,	thwart this.
Countess	⎰ Consolate ⎰ i miei desir!	Grant ⎰ me my wish!
	⎱ i miei desir!	⎱ me my wish!
	⎱ i lor desir!	⎱ them their wish!

Four times the characters repeat their earnest plea; twice Susanna's high G suspension on the word *Signor* adds a mounting urgency and a sweet insistence that would move even the Statue of the Commendatore. The Count pretends not to hear and keeps muttering that Marcellina is late. Expressing his impatience, he quickens to an undercurrent of sixteenth notes. Man to man, Figaro matches him by pleading in sixteenth notes too, setting up a patter between himself and the Count while the women continue their legato. The demands become more compelling. Finally, all four characters blend in a simple, happy-sounding resolution, the patter between the males having subsided. The Count says nothing new and the action goes on to further complexities, but Mozart has

86

revealed his deity to us. In its acceptance of the sensuous, in its pure and touching hedonism, in its poignant pleading for marital bliss or whatever lovers want, this bit of music in the second act is as religious as anything Mozart ever wrote. It voices an absolute faith in the goodness of human desire and in the holiness of sexual means of satisfying it.

This faith unites everything in *Figaro*. Though it sustains love and conventional marriage, the opera is primarily devoted to the sanctity of sensuous pleasure. And in that scene in *Don Giovanni* where the master of the sensuous enjoys a fine meal while his private orchestra regales him with lively music, it plays strands from *Figaro* as if in the service of a similar god. Both works are manifestations of the same natural piety. No one has expressed its variable character better than Mozart in these operas.

2. *Così fan tutte:* The Battle of the Sexes

In *Figaro* the feminine sex shows itself to good advantage. Despite appearances to the contrary, Susanna and the Countess are faithful to their mates through thick and thin. One feels that they have earned their final victory. Even Marcellina achieves some degree of moral stature by comparison with that worthless Bartolo who abandoned her thirty years earlier. In general, the men do not come off too well, though Figaro himself passes muster. In the face of this common threat to their sexual grandeur, the males regroup and reassert themselves. All of *Così fan tutte* is devoted to the effort.

In *Figaro* there had been no bonding of the males. They were split by political factions reflecting differences among their types of sexuality. Nor is that Rousseauistic general will, that musical oneness to which I referred, inherently masculine. As the basis for a moral community, it enables all human beings to participate inasmuch as they are equally capable of rationality. One might even say that the women of *Figaro* are more in tune with it than are the men. Even Figaro seems motivated by private interests and masculine resentment at the idea of being cuckolded rather than by a realization that no justifiable social contract could condone the Count's behavior. In *Don Giovanni*, too, there was little scope for unity among the men. They were divided by the conflict between freedom and restraint, life and death, the seducer and the Statue. The women in *Don Giovanni* do not represent a single principle either; but like the women in *Figaro* they are finally avenged against the man who seeks to dominate through sex. In this respect, the females win out in *Don Giovanni* just as in *Figaro*. In *Così* Mozart and Da Ponte present us with the dynamic opposite to these operas. They now tilt the seesaw in favor of the men.

Figaro himself had prepared us for *Così* in the aria (*Aprite un po' quegli occhi*) that asks men to open their eyes, to look at women and see what they really are. You will find, he tells his fellow males, that these so-called goddesses are but the figments of our deluded imagination. At this point in Beaumarchais there had been quite a different kind of speech. Instead of having Figaro vilify the ladies, the play gives him a political diatribe against the Count (who is not present): "Because you are a great lord, you think yourself a genius! . . . What have you done to earn so many benefits? You went to the trouble of getting born, and nothing more. Besides, as a man you're just a routine product; while I, good God!, lost in the teeming mob, I have had to use more wit and wisdom just to survive than has gone into ruling the whole Spanish Empire for the last hundred years." That is how a servant should and would speak about a master he does not respect; but obviously Mozart and Da Ponte feared the censor, himself a "routine product" of the social order. As an act of displacement, they get Figaro to vent his indignation against females in general rather than the male authority for whom it was originally intended. Women were always fair game, and no one would ever be the wiser. Figaro's fine declaration of proletarian anger thus turns into an attack on women that merely shows how stupid even the brightest of men can be.

For this, however, I blame Da Ponte more than Mozart. As it appears on the page, Figaro's aria resembles the misogyny of the Middle Ages. It even reminds us of Osmin's advice to benighted Englishmen about the rearing of their rebellious women. But when we look, or rather listen, closely, we find that the aria does something else. Through its vibrant and affirmative music, it celebrates what it also attacks. While Da Ponte's words insist that women are monsters—enchanting witches, destructive sirens, charming vixens, malicious doves, etc.—Mozart's music emphasizes the *delightfulness* of living with such rare creatures. The sensuousness of the music, its playfulness and idle repetitions, makes it impossible for men in the audience to feel indignant or women to feel insulted. Downes claims that the aria "with its stabbing accents, drastic repeated phrases and rhythms, whirling triplets and climbing pitch—can sound like the panic outburst of a man who has almost lost control of himself.["6] This interpretation seems to me unwarranted. For Mozart merges everything in the vocal line as well as the accompaniment into a rapid stream of melody that softens all intimations of resentment and makes the words sound fanciful, even funny. A "panic outburst" is unthinkable. The aria is another of Figaro's sarcastic dances about the human comedy, and thus similar to his earlier *Se vuol ballare.* To emphasize the humor and the irony in this weakness of men, who are themselves to blame for their cuckolded condition, Mozart goes so far as to introduce mocking horns in the orchestra. Bitter as the truth may be, we are forced to laugh at it.

The same attitude reappears in *Così.* In an aria that duplicates Figaro's, Guglielmo also condemns the falseness of the female; but he cannot deny that he loves the entire sex. And there is something in the recurrent "a tanti e tanti, a tanti e tanti" that suggests a marvelous versatility in women comparable to Don Giovanni's talent for seducing one person after another. In referring to the *so many* whom women have betrayed, Guglielmo's tone seems filled with the same awe and admiration that Leporello shows in the Catalogo aria. If Figaro and Guglielmo are trapped by their sexual instincts, as Masetto also was, they nevertheless enjoy their bondage. They are not medieval misogynists but rather Ovidian combatants who have reason to respect the power of the enemy. In the hands of these artful women, Guglielmo's music seems to say, we men are all as helpless as Cherubino. But what are we to do? We cannot live without women.

This preordained helplessness does not prevent Guglielmo from participating in a parable that argues for the superiority of men and condones their ultimate dominance. The parable itself exists in the mind of Don Alfonso. He is called a "philosopher," and indeed the entire opera serves to demonstrate truths about human nature which he knows in advance with absolute certainty. At no time is Don Alfonso surprised or confused or fearful of losing his bet. Though he enters into the action, he is really not a part of it. At the end, the women call him a fiend who has deceived everyone— as if he were a superannuated Don Giovanni, an aged pervert manipulating the sex lives of other people without risking his own emotions. It would be easy, therefore, to present him as a puppeteer who pulls the strings for porcelain figures that Mozart and

---

[6]Downes, "A Tender Irony," p. 12.

Da Ponte have cast in artificial postures. Most directors have mounted the opera that way—as if it were "a show of marionettes," as one critic claims.[7] But farcical as it may be, *Così* is not a comedy of dolls. To treat it as such is to diminish its moral import and to miss the point in Don Alfonso's demonstration.

In the nineteenth century it may have been necessary to protect the sensibilities of opera-goers who felt outraged by the promiscuous implications of Da Ponte's plot. Nowadays we can take more seriously the reply that Don Alfonso gives to the ladies. He says: It is true that I deceived you, but only to enlighten and undeceive. Every parable is a fiction, hence deceptive to those literal-minded people who need its message most of all. If the action is compressed into a single day, giving the ladies a remarkably short period of time to forget their fervent vows, so much the better. This may make the story less realistic, but it will give the demonstration a compelling forcefulness it could not have had otherwise. All existence in time is absurd to a philosopher like Don Alfonso. The opera is subtitled *La Scuola degli Amanti*. Don Alfonso is the professor, teaching lovers a lesson. To prove what men and women are by nature he needs only the playing time of a single performance.

What, then, is the great truth about mankind that the wise man wishes to inculcate? Certainly, it is not misogyny, at least not the hatred of women into which the lovers lapse once their sweethearts have proven faithless. Don Alfonso knows that the violence of their distress means that the men are still living in illusion. Husbands and wives may find mutual happiness, which is what he promises the reunited couples; but they must not expect perfection in each other. In short, they must not seek love in the manner of that great idealistic tradition which began with Plato and was to culminate in Romanticism. The lovers are always swearing by heaven and the stars above; but Don Alfonso swears by the earth. The philosophical bachelor is trying to bring his young friends back to terra firma, and to the truths of mundane experience.

In its courtly and neo-Platonic varieties, the idealistic tradition maintained that lovers were predestined for one another. They were united by an elective affinity such that only this man could truly love that woman, and vice versa. In the first words of the

<hr />

[7]Eric Blom, *Mozart* (New York: Pellegrini & Cudahy, 1949), p. 293. As against that kind of approach, cf. Bernard Williams, "Passion and Cynicism: Remarks on *Così fan tutte*," *Musical Times*, April 1973.

opera, Ferrando and Guglielmo insist that their sweethearts *cannot* be unfaithful ("capace non è," "tradirmi non sa"), for the very definition of love makes it impossible. Feeling as they do about the women, and knowing how the women feel for them, the young men infer that a mystical oneness must bind them to the beloved. That being so, how *could* the girls prove untrue in their affections? By showing that the women are inconstant, Don Alfonso reveals the untenability of the idealistic position. Much as he sought to disprove Berkeley by kicking a stone, Dr. Johnson had tried to ridicule the idea that love is predestined by roundly insisting there were fifty thousand people in the world—not just one—that a person could love with equal happiness. Don Alfonso upholds a similar belief, and he drives it home in a parable that *shows* the truth instead of merely asserting it.

In drawing conclusions from his demonstration, the old philosopher makes it very clear that he is condemning no one. "Everyone denounces women," he says, "but I excuse them." Why? Because that inconstancy which some people consider a vice, and others social conditioning, he recognizes as a "necessità del core"—a necessity of the heart. It is an instinct or built-in structure of femininity that makes women mutable and potentially promiscuous. *Così fan tutte*—this is how they all are—but *not* in the sense that women may therefore be attacked as false or degenerate. That was what Basilio meant in *Figaro* when he thought that he and the Count had caught Susanna in a compromising situation with Cherubino: "Così fan tutte le belle, / Non c'è alcuna novità." Don Alfonso is not saying anything of the sort, for he refuses to find any immorality in the pattern of behavior which he has disclosed. That is why he calls it a necessity of the heart. Women have variable feelings, just as men do. Whatever the poets may say, men and women are inconstant by nature. Once that lesson has been learned, we may then go on to construct a morality which enables them to live in harmony with one another. Having made his demonstration, Don Alfonso can claim in the final chorus that it is merely enlightened common sense which has shown itself. If we follow its mandates, we will find tranquillity throughout the turbulences of life.

We may also find love. For though he scorns their illusions, Don Alfonso joins the young men in a toast to the *dio d'amor*. Later, when they are prepared to consign their girlfriends to the devil, saying they can always find better fish in the sea, he convinces them that after all these are the ones they love. But the love which Don

Alfonso teaches, and which the experience of the opera makes possible, is different from the one that gripped the lovers at the beginning. Their feelings had to be changed, not merely their information about human nature. To Don Alfonso it is obvious that the delusory attitude of the lovers can only result from an unacceptable and undesirable system of emotions. "Tears, sighs, embraces, faintings away," he says in the first scene, "allow me to laugh a little." He is laughing at the idea that such behavior should be taken to indicate constancy in the women, but also he is deriding the men for carrying on in this fashion themselves. Real love involves something very different.

In the beginning the lovers value their own emotions, and the tragic outbursts of their sweethearts at the idea of departure convinces them that they will win the wager. But then the men see how easy it is to feign toward each other's beloved the same passion they initially felt toward their own. And to their astonishment, the mere playacting of passionate love has the effect of creating powerful feelings in the women. Confronted by the bogus emotionality of the Albanians, Fiordiligi and Dorabella experience passions as strong and genuine as anything they felt towards their original lovers. The fault must therefore derive from passion itself: in the men, who are deluded by it, as well as in the women, who forget their earlier vows because of it. Everything in the opera that is unnatural, strained, and comical results from passion. In the end the lovers are reunited, but it is hard to believe that they will ever feel about one another what they formerly felt. They have been sobered, disintoxicated. They may now enjoy a happy life together, but love will never be the same for them. There will be fewer palpitations.

If the young people were merely puppets, none of this would matter. Because they are real people, albeit highly stylized, they change as human beings do. Though the issue of sexual fidelity remains central to the entire work, as it is in *Figaro* and *Don Giovanni*, it leads to other and equally interesting questions. We begin to wonder about the nature of that love which Don Alfonso recommends. In *Così*, at least, Mozart and Da Ponte give us no details. They themselves were not philosophers, and perhaps we ought not to expect too much clarification from them. But in deflating the idealistic tradition and mocking the passionate, they must have had some alternative in mind. Though Don Alfonso tells us little that is positive, being a philosopher like Socrates in the negative dialogues, he and Despina think alike in most matters, and possibly he would agree with her when she says: "Love, what is it? Pleasure, comfort, appetite, joy, divertissement, pastime, contentment. It is no longer love once it becomes anxious, or troublesome and tormented, instead of pleasant." And elsewhere she gaily trills: "Amiam per comodo, per vanità"—"let us love for the pleasure of it, for the delights of vanity." This is the philosophy of the sensuous. Having ridiculed passion, Mozart and Da Ponte would seem to leave us with little else.

Sensuousness belongs to feminine as well as masculine sexuality. If the opera is advocating it as the only acceptable standard, it may also legislate equality between the sexes. But Mozart and Da Ponte will not go that far. The division between male and female is more sharply drawn in *Così* than in any of the other Mozart operas. Nowhere else are the men and women segregated so constantly into their own duets and trios. Almost all of the intersexual ensembles express conflicting sentiments. And as in *Don Giovanni*, it is often the conflict between the sensuous and the passionate that structures the music. This is most evident in the tumultuous finale to Act I, where the women are shouting like furies while the men are chortling with delight. Usually, however, the conflict is presented more subtly. Near the beginning of the first act, Mozart uses it to achieve an effect of ambiguous tenderness. While the four lovers sing a passionate sequence of *Addio*'s, Don Alfonso keeps telling us that if this goes on he will die of laughter. Once the men have left, Don Alfonso's powers of persuasion descend upon the two girls, and as a trio they sing another of Mozart's quasi-religious paeans to the goodness of the sensuous. In music that turns this parting into the sweetest of sorrows, they implore whatever gods there be for gentle winds and tranquil waves and "every benign element responsive to our desire."

But such unison is rare in *Così*. Only at the very end does everyone sing together harmoniously. Even there we know that ultimate peace cannot last for long, and it is just as well that the curtain quickly falls. For though the sensuous triumphs, in the female as well as the male, the power struggle continues as before.

The parable itself presupposes a tyranny of the men which can only lead to sexual war. Don Alfonso is clearly partisan to male supremacy. However philosophical he may be, he never doubts the legitimacy of the wager. The men blandly assume that they have a *right* to test the feelings of the beloved in any way they wish, as a scientist has the right to experiment with nature. And although the women complain at the end that Don Alfonso deceived them, we all know that Ferrando and Guglielmo participated freely in the plot. They agree to the wager as a means of defending the virtue of their ladies; but the wager itself involves trickery and falsification that only a Don Giovanni could relish. In fact, if we eliminate their final sop to marital convention, the two young men fit perfectly into the myth of Don Juan. Not only do they assert the freedom of action—testing and not being tested—which belongs to male dominance, but also they play at disguises, exchange fiancées so that each of them is making love to a woman he does not love, and declare themselves victors once they have brought the woman to the point of seduction.

In some ways, Ferrando and Guglielmo illustrate the Don Juan character *better* than Don Giovanni. For in their lovemaking they sound and act as if they were really carried away by the emotions they are presumably feigning. With his friend's mistress, each of them is the same fond lover he was in the first act singing to and about his own beloved. And surely no one could seduce as many women as Don Juan does unless *something* of the sort happened to him each time. In Don Giovanni nothing ever does. He has only a passionate desire to seduce. Ferrando and Guglielmo outdo him in feeling authentic passion, even for each other's girlfriend. At least, this is what the opera encourages us to believe. In *Don Giovanni* we are required to believe the opposite.

The young men also differ from Don Giovanni in another aspect important to male psychology: they compete against each other. Don Giovanni is in a category by himself. In Tirso's play, he is one among many youths who go about seducing women. In the opera, however, there is no competition in his erotic sport. Leporello keeps the catalogue for everyone's edification, and we are all vastly impressed by Don Giovanni's machismo; but really he has no one to vie against. Ferrando and Guglielmo have each other. They are comrades in arms, each striving to exceed the other. Why else would they switch women in carrying out the wager? To avoid detection? Possibly. Because it is unthinkable to deceive the woman you love? Very likely. But also, they are testing their own virility—not merely, as they say, proving the fidelity of their sweethearts. They are like little boys who play at seeing who can urinate farthest. When it looks as if Fiordiligi has remained constant to Guglielmo while Dorabella has betrayed Ferrando, Guglielmo naturally assumes he is the better man. Don Alfonso seconds him in this, knowing that it will force Ferrando to compete even harder. Male sexuality being linked to the need for aggressive achievement, Don

Giovanni grabs one woman after another and brings Leporello along to keep accounts. The lovers in *Così* are more intimately related to one another. They each test the other's ability to succeed with two women at once, only one of whom they really love and want to marry. In losing to Don Alfonso, both lovers succeed in their competition against each other. The women are declared faithless, but possibly they would not be forgiven as quickly as they are if the men were not so thoroughly pleased by their success as ravaging males.

So deep is the masculine need to prove one's sexual prowess that hardly any cruelty will deter it. When Ferrando and Guglielmo go off to war, they elicit suffering in the women that we experience as comical because we know the actual situation and have agreed to suspend our usual moral categories. In exaggerating passionate outbursts, the music parodies all tragic leave-takings; and though the women threaten suicide now that they are losing their lovers, we assume they will do themselves no injury. This is not the Dido myth: we rightly foresee a succession of new sensations rather than a termination in death. Nevertheless, it is essential that the women really feel grief, for that enforces the theme of mutability when their emotions change later on. And indeed, the weeping of the women is duplicated by sobs in the orchestra that sound utterly sincere. It is just that we must not *concern* ourselves with their suffering, and so we too become a party to the sexual cruelty.

In relation to the suffering of the men, however, we are expected to respond quite differently. When they undergo a kind of joint cuckoldry in the second act, both the music and the text insist upon our sympathy. Ferrando's tormented aria *Tradito, schernito* is one of the most passionate Mozart ever wrote. In general, what the men do to the women is only a joke, the cruelty is not "real" cruelty, the entire escapade is just an innocent way of proving that the women are perfect, etc., etc. But what the women do to the *men,* in ignorance and subject to the unrelenting machinations of Despina as well as Don Alfonso, shocks and dismays and causes sorrowful adjustments throughout the moral perspective. The women are vilified by their lovers, who take them back under conditions that afford the men an even greater dominance than before. The women themselves cringe like recognized criminals and promise to make amends in acts of sexual submission. The males march off as conquering heroes, never apologizing for anything they have done. On the contrary, they act as if their suffering proves that only they are capable of love. When the women insist that now they will know how to adore their rightful husbands, the men smugly reply that, yes, they do believe in their devotion "ma la prova io far non vo' "—"but I wouldn't want to prove it." Such condescension, such grudging faith, and from men who came off rather badly in the test just completed! One can only hope that after the curtain has fallen, the young ladies whisper to each other, "Men are like that." *Così fan tutti.* How sad it would be if the women really thought the men are any better than they!

In *Figaro* and *Don Giovanni* the battle between the sexes is never clearly drawn. In both of these operas the male predator comes to grief, but through other males as well as the females. In *Così*, however, the sexes are separated into two opposing camps, and the military symbolism pervades throughout. The men depart at the beginning and return at the end to the music of drums and fifes; the women try to kill themselves with their lovers' swords; and Fiordiligi even seeks to flee temptation in her lover's uniform. Each camp has its shock troops, and each has its high command. But in this game of sexual war, the match has been fixed. The men have seen to it that they cannot lose to the women, even though the lovers lose to Don Alfonso. For Despina, the general on the feminine side, is in the pay of the enemy.

As a defender of women's liberation in sex, Despina casts aspersions on male fidelity just as Don Alfonso had done vis-à-vis the females. But unlike Don Alfonso, she can hardly be considered a philosopher. She is only a servant, and in her first entrance she grumbles about her lot much as Leporello does. Her playgirl morality looks interesting on paper, but the high and flimsy melody she sings assures us that she is far from being a deep thinker. She tells women to lie, to feign coquettishly, to flatter and deceive. She has the mind and the music of an inferior being, suitable perhaps for diversionary tactics but wholly incapable of helping women advance towards the more fruitful pleasures of life. She is no more a philosopher than she is a physician or lawyer—two other roles she enacts to comic effect. But worst of all, Despina's pronouncements are always tainted by the fact that she panders her wit to anyone who offers money. Though she is not in on the wager and cannot know that her efforts towards liberation will actually lead the women into further subjugation, she continually commits sexual treason. With leaders like her, how can the women possibly win?

As if to compensate for the sexual imbalance, Mozart creates in Fiordiligi a character who is more fascinating and more profound than all the men put together. When she tries to run away, it is

Despina who betrays her, and fittingly so. For how could Despina understand the soul of a woman who may yield to what she herself considers shameful but will not lie about it (Despina's recommendation for every crisis indiscriminately)? Fiordiligi cannot stand against the bigger battalions of the young men. They are professional soldiers who ruthlessly pursue each advantage, and she has never learned how to survive in such a world. But she fights valiantly for what she believes in. Though the others change throughout the opera, only she really develops as a person.

Fiordiligi is obviously the older of the two sisters. Dorabella defers to her on more than one occasion. In making Dorabella a mezzo-soprano, Mozart gives her some of the earthiness that nineteenth-century composers were to carry even further for voices with her kind of coloring. For Fiordiligi, however, Mozart demands a soprano with a large variability of register, capable of ranging from very high high notes to very low lows. Moreover, the two extremes seem to exist independently of one another, as if Fiordiligi contained two female voices within her. And in a sense she does, for she is a divided woman both psychologically and musically. The highs and the lows do not always mean the same, but they always signify a split between the two aspects of Fiordiligi's personality. It is as if she cannot harmonize the head and the chest voices. Though the psychiatric terminology may not be very helpful, one can detect in her musical self-presentation a tendency to schizophrenia. In a way that may be relevant to Fiordiligi, one otolaryngologist speculates about voices as follows: "Increased head register means lyrical in the field of singing. Increased chest register means dramatic. . . . Schizophrenics separate these registers into two different voice patterns which they can use alternately."[8]

The first time we see this is in the aria *Come scoglio*. It follows upon a moving recitative in which Fiordiligi informs the intruding Albanians that nothing can shake the sisters from their fidelity to the departed lovers. Having said this quite convincingly, with fluent support from the believing orchestra, Fiordiligi then launches into an aria that advances the message not a bit but rephrases it in the most diverse manner. At times it soars to great sublimity, as in the words "nella fede e nell'amor," but at other times it makes the very idea of constancy look like an empty notion that no one could truly believe. When she compares herself to a

[8]Paul J. Moses, *The Voice of Neurosis* (New York: Grune & Stratton, 1954), p. 48.

rock, mentions the winds and the tempest against which she will remain unmoved, and specifies death as the only thing that could have any effect on her changeless devotion, the voice is either too high or too low. As if to detach itself from so strange a person, the orchestra starts making parodistic noises. For the most part, however, the effect remains ambiguous; and out of context, the aria can be made to sound magnificent in its fervent declamation. But then just as the soprano is beginning to seduce us with the drama of her delivery and the agility of her coloratura, Mozart undercuts it all by having her trill the crucial words about the unchanging feelings in her heart. The trill is itself a quick oscillation, and it alone would tell us that this woman's sentiments are less constant than she thinks, that in fact they are capable of changing rapidly.[9]

In mingling the sublime and the ridiculous, *Come scoglio* reminds one of what Berlioz said in claiming that Donna Anna's *Non mi dir* degenerates into buffoonery. Though I believe Berlioz was wrong about Donna Anna's aria, I feel that his words do apply to Fiordiligi's—except that Mozart knew exactly what he was doing, and did it to perfection. *Non mi dir* is not comic; but *Come scoglio* can certainly be taken that way. And yet, Fiordiligi herself is not a clown. She obviously wishes to live up to the noble sentiments that the music also embodies. Her aria is farcical, and the coloratura extravagances a bit of buffoonery, simply because Mozart refuses to let us believe in the feasibility of such ideals. Human beings are not rocks who stand against the winds and the tempest. Their sentiments do not remain constant, and normally they do not expect them to. Only a deluded idealist like Fiordiligi, pure of heart but pitifully naïve, could hope for anything of the sort. She is filled with the grandeur of her aspiration, and the great aria conveys this; but if she knew here what she does at the end of the opera, she would realize that she is making a fool of herself. Her moral goals far exceed her actual capability. Her vocal line registers the disparity throughout the aria. She can never merge the head and the chest. She is only the parody of a tragic heroine.

To some extent, Mozart prepared us for *Come scoglio* in the oath that Fiordiligi and Dorabella had taken swearing that love

---

[9]On Mozart's ambiguity in *Come scoglio*, see Stanley Sadie, *Mozart* (New York: Grossman, 1970), p. 160. Cf. also Eric Blom, "The Music of the Opera," in *Mozart's Così Fan Tutte* by Edward J. Dent, Eric Blom, and Clemence Dane (London: John Lane, 1946), p. 35.

must visit unending pain upon them if their heartfelt desires should ever change. The words are solemn, but the girls sing them to light and even frivolous music. Later Dorabella sings an impassioned aria, *Smanie implacabili che m'agitate*, which walks a tightrope between straight *opera seria* and a parody of it. Once we have heard *Come scoglio*, however, we retroactively distrust Dorabella's authenticity as well. And in fact, the rest of her music in the opera generally comes through as sensuous rather than passionate, even in the love scenes.

In expressing high ideals through Fiordiligi but then reviling them in the very act of presentation, Mozart shows a streak of cruelty reminiscent of Don Giovanni. He compensates for it by giving Fiordiligi another great aria, and this time he reveals her divided personality through music that is wholly sympathetic to her as a person. The aria *Per pietà, ben mio* has few extreme contrasts compared to *Come scoglio*, though it still shows the soprano as a woman of two voices. Now, however, she is not enunciating ideals of conduct, but rather begging her absent lover to forgive her if she actually succumbs to the seductive Albanian. Her high voice is therefore not as high as before, and it sings with an intimate warmth that is touching as well as beautiful. Nor does Mozart ridicule the tender sentiments Fiordiligi expresses. He even sustains them with hearty French horns that make us feel the lover she is singing to is good-natured and will understand how much he really means to her. Fiordiligi appeals to him as a way of reawakening the image of their love. But then her voice keeps dropping far down as she realizes what her new infatuation portends. She feels herself descending into the uncontrollable depths of sexuality. Her yearning for the distant beloved is strong and mellifluous, but wholly incapable of saving her. The two voices alternate, despite her conscious desire to remain faithful. She cannot repress her instinctual drives, the erotic impulse cannot be dissipated by memories of the past or hopes for the future, and we know that she will never resolve her conflict.

Though this aria is addressed to her rightful lover, it foreshadows the moment when Fiordiligi tells the Albanian to "do with me as you wish." She yields to the invader as one who can no longer fight her own weaknesses. When she surrenders, it is like a great oak falling in the forest. We suffer with her, and so does Mozart. When Fiordiligi condemns her own frailty in the recitative before *Per pietà, ben mio*, the orchestra sighs with unmistakable sympathy; throughout her desperate appeal for help, it tries to remind her of pleasures with the real beloved; and when her last resistance crumbles, it supports her as best it can.

In *Figaro* there is no character like Fiordiligi. Neither Susanna nor the Countess have her combination of strength and debility. In a sense, they are more shallow characters. We learn more details about them, but we do not get to know them in greater depth. They are inherently more simplistic. Though Susanna and the Countess engage in deceptions, or at least dubious practices, they seem to be relatively unconcerned about the implications of their behavior. They never condemn themselves, nor have they much reason to. Their sense of rectitude may help them to subdue the Count, but it makes them morally less interesting than Fiordiligi. Moreover, as I have suggested, they have little to tell us about the nature of passion. Fiordiligi tells us a great deal—as much perhaps as Elvira, whom she resembles in being inwardly divided, in fighting unsuccessfully against the love she feels, and in suffering from erotic desires that will never bring her happiness. As if to balance Despina's gay description of the sensuous, Fiordiligi speaks of her own passionate involvement as "madness, torture, remorse, suffering, folly, perfidy, and emotional betrayal." It is here that the orchestra sighs. Mozart has made his point about the danger and the dreadful joy of passion. He could never have done so with the women in *Figaro*.

Fiordiligi is morally more interesting than Susanna or the Countess in other ways as well. As if she were the Biblical character of the same name, Susanna fends off the dirty old men who come in the person of the Count and his henchman Basilio; but though society benefits from her struggle against the *droit du seigneur,* she does not appear as a female hero. For her part, the Countess wins back her husband through her constancy and patience, as if she were a modern version of saintly Griselda, but she too achieves a victory that is personal rather than heroic. As a combatant within a battle between the sexes, Fiordiligi opens more glorious possibilities to the imagination. She does not exploit them, but she is a woman who feels things deeply and who suffers for her feelings. Though she fails to achieve it, the *ideal* of female fidelity lives in her more vividly than in either of the other women.

In the first scene of *Così,* Don Alfonso says that woman's fidelity is like the phoenix: everyone speaks of it, but no one knows where to find it. As a thing of flight and soaring aspiration that rises from the burning ashes in which it is consumed, the phoenix may well symbolize human passion. Certainly D. H. Lawrence took it as such. Fiordiligi is a rare bird precisely of that sort. She is first reborn, somewhat diminished, as Pamina in *The Magic Flute,* and then resplendently, as Leonore in *Fidelio.* Beethoven even imitated *Per pietà, ben mio* in Leonore's *Abscheulicher* aria, using three obbligato horns instead of two.[10] And yet, one feels that Beethoven could not have appreciated the greatness of Fiordiligi as a mythic character. If he had, he would not have criticized Mozart for writing such an "immoral" opera.

3. Mozart's Solution in *The Magic Flute*

The three Italian operas that Mozart wrote with Da Ponte end with the promise of sexual harmony. As in the final scene between Ottavio and Donna Anna, the last line of *Così* refers to the "bella calma" that will ensue for the lovers; and after their *giorno di tormenti,* the characters of Figaro announce that now they will all be *contenti.* Since peace and contentment is what few people find in life, these happy endings are not insignificant. But as achievements for the human spirit, they do not penetrate very deeply. The sensuous life is a surface phenomenon. It cannot tolerate the yearning, the frustration, the pain that belongs to the passionate. In their ambivalence towards passion, the Da Ponte operas tend to subordinate it to the goods that sensuousness provides.

To think about human relations as a battle between the sexes is already to dispose one's outlook towards the sensuous. The metaphor itself creates a distance from the reality of sexual conflict that enables us to treat it somewhat lightly. It is not fortuitous that Ovid, who understands little more than the sensuous, should make the battle between the sexes his major theme. We know that male and female do not fight exactly in the way that warriors do; but thinking of their interpersonal skirmishes, their physical and psychological confrontations, as moments of warfare enables us to *play* with the implications of sexual intimacy. And once we are playing with sexuality, we are already participating in the sensuous. To understand the passionate, we must realize how serious it is to those who live through the agony and the ecstasy. Lucretius, who scarcely concerns himself with the sensuous, sees passion as a murderous calamity, a disease, a terrible suffering that must be elimi-

[10]On this, see Einstein, *Mozart,* p. 446.

nated immediately, not played with or falsified through fanciful metaphors. He may not understand human nature better than Ovid, but he cuts deeper—in the sense in which a surgeon might.

In the final months of his life, Mozart seemed to have felt the need for this deeper penetration. Though the Da Ponte operas are not wholly frivolous, they make frivolity into a positive virtue without giving equal importance to many other virtues. *Così* closes with the philosopher's plea for reasonableness, but the morality that this entails is never clearly stated. In *The Magic Flute* Mozart returns to the concept of reason, capitalizes it as befits the German language, and fills it with the aura of his newly found Masonic religion. But though *The Magic Flute* was not, could not have been, written in collaboration with Da Ponte, it presupposes many of the same problems as the Italian operas. The whole question of male dominance remains, and it is answered in ways that do not contradict the earlier operas. In *The Magic Flute,* as in the Da Ponte operas, male supremacy is stated as a fundamental rule of nature. The mythology of the work largely consists in its affirmation.

Scholars have made much of the fact that Pamina leads Tamino through the cavern of fire while he plays his magic flute. The cavern of fire may well symbolize the hazards of sexual intercourse; the flute surely signifies the magical virility of music; and the entire scene can be taken as an idealization of women who lead men upwards through love. Pamina herself says: "I shall always / Be your true companion. / I lead you myself, / And love guides me on." We shall return to the mythic elements in this situation; but from the outset, I wish to emphasize that *The Magic Flute* never accords the female an heroic mission comparable to the male's. Writers like Kerman are mistaken when they claim that Mozart made Pamina's uplifting influence "the center of his drama."[11] Even her growth as a person is only secondary in *The Magic Flute,* which remains throughout a fable about masculine potency. It begins as a typical adventure of the questing male, who must use his cunning and courage as a man to win the imprisoned female. It ends with her becoming a holy grail through whom he finds salvation beyond his earlier expectations. From beginning to end, it is the *male* who must conquer reality. In doing so, he asserts his mystical dominance as nowhere else in the Mozart operas.

For the first part of *The Magic Flute,* Mozart was able to draw upon the simplified perspectives of his earlier work *The Abduction*

[11]Kerman, *Opera as Drama,* p. 125.

from the Seraglio. There the prince, as the wholesome lover, the fine and gentle male, penetrates the palace where the beloved is kept prisoner by a different kind of man: crude and comically gross in the person of Osmin, semi-oriental and possibly sadistic in the case of the Pasha, who threatens to force his love upon the proud beauty. The opera ends with the Pasha's proving himself to be merciful, much more humane than his western counterparts. He is even concerned that the true lovers should be free to marry one another, just as the conventional-minded audience wishes.

The first act of *The Magic Flute* duplicates all this on a higher level. Having fallen in love with the image of Pamina, the prince undertakes to liberate her from Sarastro. By the end of the first act, Tamino learns that Sarastro is good, not evil; a noble priest, not a tyrant; in fact, a man who wishes to sanctify Tamino's love for Pamina. Sarastro resembles the Pasha in being carried onstage to the accompaniment of a march, in acting like a potentate, in feeling personally wounded at the idea that the princess he has captured but in no way maltreated should want to escape, and in enunciating the highest of moral standards. Osmin has his equivalent in the lecherous Monostatos; the good-hearted servant Pedrillo is recreated as Papageno. If *The Magic Flute* had ended there, it would have been a superior version of *The Abduction* but not much more.

The Magic Flute does not end with the first act, however, because the rest is needed as a clarification of what has been going on—not only in this opera but also in Mozart's ideological development as a whole. Had he lived longer, Mozart might have transcended the ideas in *The Magic Flute;* but as it is, they provide a moment of resolution for the problems about love and sexuality that beset him in the earlier works. In the operas written with Da Ponte, Mozart sounds like a man who does not really believe in love between the sexes—at least, not love as a unique and lasting oneness in which each participant unselfishly devotes himself to the welfare of the other. In *Don Giovanni* only Ottavio and Donna Anna could possibly qualify as true lovers in this sense, and their union is blighted by a supervening struggle between life and death—Don Giovanni vs. the Commendatore—that makes their relationship seem rather uninteresting. In *Figaro* the Countess, Susanna, and even Figaro may be loving persons; but the opera is intriguing, and forever depends upon the phenomenon of intrigue, because we can never be certain that anyone in it really loves anyone else. In *Così* the philosophical demonstration tends to indicate that love is not a human possibility at all, unless we reinterpret it as an easy-going arrangement that enables men and women to live together without expecting too much of one another. In these three Italian operas there is no such thing as complete, harmonious, innocent (but also passionate) love. On the contrary, the drama is always generated by difficulties internal to each couple such that we can never know whether they are truly in love. Even after the happy endings of *Così* and *Figaro,* and despite the benign promise of their multiple marriages, we cannot be sure that human beings are capable of authentic oneness of this sort.

This characteristic of the Da Ponte operas is epitomized by the duet between Susanna and the Count in which she dissembles submission to his demands, but does so through a confusion of yes's and no's. For at a very deep level of her being, Susanna is indeed confused. While tricking the Count, she also reveals that even she—a bright, good-hearted girl who will not treat Figaro the way that Zerlina or Despina would—does not know what she really feels. Can she be certain that she loves Figaro? In the face of temptation, is her love as strong as she would like it to be? Is she sure that Figaro loves her with the firmness and the constancy that she desires? Possibly yes, possibly no: she vacillates. In hinting at this effect, Da Ponte goes far beyond Beaumarchais; but it is only in the sensuous ambiguities of Mozart's music for the duet that one sees the pervasive uncertainty. Nor do any of the other characters in the Da Ponte operas understand their erotic feelings—with the exception of Don Giovanni and Don Alfonso, who do not believe in love.

In *The Abduction* and *The Magic Flute,* however, the situation is totally different. These operas (both singspiele and both in German) presuppose a marvelous unity between the lovers. The drama arises not from them but from the hostility of the external world, which cannot tolerate the ideality of their love. Though the lovers are one and spiritually inseparable, reality imposes material interferences. It separates them physically. It sets up obstacles that seek to alienate them, to weaken their oneness, to prevent them from living together or joining forces. But despite all trials, the lovers win out; and they do so because nothing can finally negate the inherent indivisibility of their love. They make an eternal pair in a way that none of the Da Ponte characters do. Reality must either destroy the pair or else accept it as a unit. In the end, reality submits, and we realize that we have been watching a fable rather than a dramatic comedy. The same is true of *Fidelio,* Beethoven's singspiel, though it differs from Mozart's German operas in ways that we shall see.

The Magic Flute provides a resolution to Mozart's treatment of love and sexuality by continuing the genre of *The Abduction* but filling it with insights that grew with the intervening operas. Since Mozart had the whole story of *The Abduction* altered before he would work on the music and then ten years later collaborated very closely with Schikaneder on the text of *The Magic Flute*, the development from one to the other must surely indicate a growth in Mozart himself.[12]

In *The Abduction* Mozart was prepared to assert the ideality of love, but he would not face up to the possibility of conflict between the passionate and the sensuous. In fact, each is given its own place in the opera, its own music, its own characters, its own autonomous domain. The categories scarcely overlap or coexist in any single character, and they never oppose each other within a character. Thus Belmonte and Constanze are not only true lovers inwardly united despite outside opposition, but also they are individually defined as passionate beings. Pedrillo, Osmin, and Blonde (Constanze's maid) are purely sensuous in matters of love, even though Osmin becomes violent in his hatred of Pedrillo and Belmonte. The Pasha begins as a passionate lover but then gives way before the superior passion of Belmonte. Neither the Pasha nor Belmonte nor Constanze—all of them rulers and aristocrats—shows inclinations towards sensuous sexuality. They are highly cultivated people, and with his interest in gardening and architecture the Pasha would seem to appreciate the wider aesthetic possibilities of sensory pleasure. But in lovemaking, the three principals leave the sensuous to their servants.

In disposing of the two aspects of sexuality by reference to this social hierarchy, Mozart is obviously elevating the passionate above the sensuous in a way that none of his Italian operas could accept. He was partly adhering to a theatrical convention; but the letter to his father dated September 26, 1781, indicates the importance Mozart gave to his passionate love music in *The Abduction*. Of Bel-

---

[12]In *The Tenth Muse*, Patrick J. Smith points out that *The Abduction* is "traditionally considered the starting point of German operatic music of consequence" (pp. 249–50); but he fails to see its importance for *The Magic Flute*, whose libretto he calls an "elevated hodgepodge" (p. 186) and "Schikaneder's farrago" (p. 250). Dent too considered *The Magic Flute*'s libretto "a mere agglomeration of absurdities" (*Mozart's Operas*, p. 222).

monte's aria *O wie ängstlich, o wie feurig* ("Oh, how anxious, oh, how fervid"), he says: "Would you like to know how I have expressed it—and even indicated his throbbing heart? By the two violins playing octaves. . . . You feel the trembling—the faltering—you see how his throbbing heart begins to swell; this I have expressed by a crescendo. You hear the whispering and the sighing—which I have indicated by the first violins with mutes and a flute playing in unison."[13] Mozart obviously feels that in Belmonte's aria he has caught the spirit of the passionate; and in the music, as in his letter, he treats it with an unambiguous acceptance that rarely occurs in his later work.

In separating the sensuous and the passionate as it does, *The Abduction* lacks the organic unity one finds in the greater operas of Mozart. Having segregated the characters as either noble and therefore passionate or else servile and therefore sensuous, it strings together two series of arias: one for each aspect of sexuality. Within this structure, Mozart is ingenious and quite analytical; for he carefully arranges that each aria shall explore a different facet of either the passionate or the sensuous. When Belmonte first enters, he sings the aria *Hier soll ich dich denn sehen* ("Here may I hope to see you") in order to identify himself as a passionate lover yearning for an absent beloved whom he must rescue. He is immediately countered by Osmin's sensuous air *Wer ein Liebchen hat gefunden* ("He who has found a beloved"). Like Belmonte, Osmin is lamenting the fact that he does not have the woman he wants; but with the grotesque softness of a eunuch, Osmin sings a poignant but rather comical tune that is certainly not fervent. All the while, he stands on a ladder picking the fruit of a fig tree. What could be more sensuous, or more suggestive of the fleshly delights to be found in a Turkish harem?

Later in the act, Belmonte sings the passionate aria discussed in Mozart's letter. The hope of seeing Constanze seems about to be realized. His ardor and anxiety are almost feverish, as if nothing less can overcome the dangers Osmin portrays in his aria about punishing those who cross him. Despite its unruliness, there is something very sensuous even in this aria of Osmin's. For Mozart conveys the idea that Osmin takes a lascivious pleasure in imagining the hanging, the burning, the beheading of an enemy. When the Pasha later threatens Constanze with all the arts of torture if

---

[13]*The Letters of Mozart and His Family*, II, 769.

she refuses to yield, he sounds truly angry, like a man who does feel passion. In him it is permissible.

In her prolonged resistance to the Pasha, Constanze sings one passionate aria after another. First she reminisces in a heartbroken but nostalgic way about her love for Belmonte. Then she vents all the sadness of her present condition. Later she defiantly chooses pain and torture rather than submit to a man she does not love. Can one envisage Susanna singing *Martern aller Arten* to the Count? Or any other woman in the Da Ponte operas? The notion jars; it is not wholly congruous to the concept of love in these works. *Come scoglio* comes closest to being a comparable aria, except that by design it parodies and ridicules the very idea of martyrdom or rocklike resistance to the alien suitor. Only if one fully believes in the passionate can anything as dramatic and vehement as *Martern aller Arten* have an effect that is not comical. It succeeds in *The Abduction* because Constanze has been created as the exemplar of true love and genuine passion in the female. She has no other being.

As the representatives of sensuousness in a sexual union, Pedrillo and Blonde sing only light, witty, and tuneful music. Blonde coquettishly informs Osmin that women must be won through flattery and beguilement. Later she uses the music of a hornpipe to express the gaiety of escaping by sea, just as Pedrillo sings a delightful and equally superficial romanza to the accompaniment of plucking strings. Even Pedrillo's *Frisch zum Kampfe! Frisch zum Streite!* is more mock-heroic than anything else, as he playfully beats his chest and pretends to feel a courage that lies beyond his station.

On the other hand, the sensuous little people do participate in the two quartets of joyous love. Since each couple symbolizes a different kind of sexuality, the quartet music harmonizes both ardor and delight, both passion and the sensuous. The first quartet occurs when the lovers meet before trying to escape. It expels the tension that has been building up through the passionate arias of Belmonte and Constanze, and it gives Pedrillo and Blonde an opportunity to savor the immediate goodness of a happy reconciliation. The second act ends with this ecstatic music of reunion. In the letter previously cited, Mozart describes the clamorous finale of the first act as a device to "wind up with a great deal of noise, which is always appropriate at the end of an act. The more noise the better, and the shorter the better, so that the audience may not have time to cool down with their applause." Would he say the same about the quartet at the end of the second act? For him, was the harmonizing of sensuous and passionate just a theatrical trick? Who can tell?

In the third act, the two couples are captured by Osmin, and the principal lovers must face the prospect of summary execution. They respond with the moving duet *Welch' ein Geschick! O Qual der Seele!* ("What a fate! O torment of the soul!"). Through its impassioned music they have already overcome the death that awaits them. For in ways that Wagner was to exploit much further, passion makes lovers impervious to dying. The Pasha can destroy Belmonte and Constanze, but he cannot impair their oneness. When the Pasha realizes the impregnability of this love, he yields to it, forfeits his own passion, and releases the four prisoners. The second quartet then bursts out with the joyfulness of final consummation. In it the passionate and the sensuous seem harmonized to a degree that is unmatched in any of the other Mozart operas.

I have suggested that Pasha Selim anticipates Sarastro in being a good man rather than a tyrant as one expected. Actually, the bond between these characters is even closer. *The Abduction* is able to reach its happy ending only after the Pasha undergoes a spiritual transformation that puts him in the same condition as Sarastro. In a sense, Sarastro begins in *The Magic Flute* where Pasha Selim ends in *The Abduction*. Having learned that Belmonte is the son of his worst enemy, a Christian invader who acted unjustly towards him in the past, the Pasha is at first disposed to take his revenge through the captives. Constanze's courage in offering to die with her lover causes him to relent. Releasing the woman that he loves but finally refuses to possess against her will, he enunciates the highest principle of all enlightened government in the eighteenth century: "If one cannot prevail through benevolence, one must leave other people alone [literally, "get off their backs"]."

All this reappears in the thinking of Sarastro, who seems to rule his ecclesiastic society with an absolute power similar to the Pasha's. Though the Queen of the Night is finally destroyed by some cataclysm as she and her cohorts invade the sacred halls, Sarastro insists that vengeance is unknown there. We are a long way from Bartolo and the Count, or even from Donna Anna and the Commendatore. We are also, perhaps, a long way from what Mozart wrote in a letter shortly before he composed *The Abduction*: "If anyone offends me I must revenge myself, and unless I revenge myself with interest I consider I have only repaid my enemy and not corrected him."[14] Mozart takes the Pasha beyond his own capability; and through Sarastro he suggests that society as a whole may surmount the need for revenge that even a genius can hardly resist.

Even more important, the Pasha transcends both the sensuous and the passionate much as Sarastro will. Though he loves Constanze with a melancholy passion, we also associate him with the sensuous. He is the lord of this languorous and exotic land, and he arrives to the titillating music of the Janissary guards. We also know he keeps a harem, as if he were a Turkish Don Giovanni. And yet, he foregoes both types of sexuality in an attitude of self-abnegation. It is this transcendence that *The Magic Flute* renews, expanding it into a way of life which Sarastro typifies but which eventually includes the lovers as well.

This rebirth to a new and more spiritual love is symbolized by the magic flute itself. As they give it to Tamino in the first act, the three ladies of the Queen of the Night tell him that now he has the power to transform all human passions ("der Menschen Leidenschaft verwandeln"). He can bring joy to those who are sad and love to those who would otherwise be without it. The three ladies may possibly mean that the magic flute satisfies and even creates the passionate; but as the action progresses, we learn that their queen embodies the weaknesses and irrationalities of passion which the lovers must learn to overcome. The flute helps them to do so—without, however, leading them into sensuous alternatives.

It is by giving this magical power to the flute, the male instrument which the man uses to express his creative heroism, that *The Magic Flute* returns to the erotic problems of the Da Ponte operas. For though we cannot doubt that Tamino and Pamina are ideal lovers, the hostility which they face from the external world involves the war between the sexes. The conflict between the Queen of the Night and Sarastro becomes a struggle for power between the forces of darkness and the forces of light—with all that this means in relation to eighteenth-century metaphors of enlightenment. Tamino is sent into the world of adventure by the matriarchal Queen of the Night, just as all men are brought into being by a mother. He emancipates himself from her through the society of pure-hearted, civilized men whom Sarastro rules as a holy patriarch. Though devoted to her daughter, the mother-figure is irrational, wilful, and murderous in her self-preferment. The father-

---

[14]June 20, 1781, in *The Letters of Mozart and His Family,* II, 747.

figure is wise, patient, and serenely powerful. George Bernard Shaw spoke better than he knew when he said that Mozart gave Sarastro music that would be suitable even for God to sing. For without the benefit of orthodoxy, without anything more doctrinal than the pagan mummery of the Freemasons, Sarastro serves as an incarnation of that heavenly Father whom the western world calls God. Tamino fulfills his quest as a man by aligning himself with this kindred male spirit. By undergoing the rites of initiation, he prevents the wicked witch-mother from sullying the perfection of his love for her daughter. Even the magic flute, given to him by the Queen of the Night, turns out to have been constructed by Pamina's wonder-working father. The opera ends with the rays of the sun chasing away the night, with masculine authority asserting itself over the subversive charms of the feminine. The world is thus purified, and the fated lovers may live happily ever after.

Throughout his mission and in all his trials, Tamino remains courageous. Papageno, the natural man who is merely sensuous, does not; and neither does Pamina. They both waver and even attempt suicide. Though Mozart gives them the magnificent duet to love *Wir wollen uns der Liebe freu'n, / Wir leben durch die Lieb' allein,* he also knows that unaided they cannot achieve the goal they desire. Papageno is weak, and Pamina loses heart when Tamino will not talk to her, communication with women being forbidden by the priests. Only the intervention of the Three Boys prevents her from killing herself. They have been sent by the Queen of the Night to guide Tamino; but once they reach Sarastro's domain, they seem to join forces with him. Hovering overhead, they are the Mozartian god of love in his final transformation, sexless cherubim, Cherubino without his carnal appetite. They save Pamina by assuring her that Tamino's love is unshakeable, just as they save Papageno by showing him how to get his Papagena. When Pamina says that she will lead Tamino since Love itself guides her on, we must remember that she has been directed by the Three Boys who symbolize love. But in being boys, they also signify the inherent innocence of the male. In contrast to the three ladies of the Queen of the Night, who are brazen and competitive, the Three Boys are pure. Perhaps that is why they are able to lead Tamino to Sarastro in the first place. Being a mere female, Pamina could not survive without masculine support, and neither could she show Tamino the way to their salvation. As Sarastro informs Pamina in a crucial speech in the first act which prepares us for everything that happens in the second, "Only a man should guide your feelings. / Without him every woman is likely / To wander beyond her proper sphere."

At the same time, women are not to be victimized or seduced. They are only to be put in their place as helpmates within the scheme of things. The Queen of the Night sinks into the earth at the end, but her daughter joins the holy band. Pamina walks through the fire as an imperfect creature for the sake of whom men must make themselves perfect. The same is even true of Papagena, that birdlike daughter of nature who can only think of endlessly propagating the species. When Papageno forgets that he must not talk to women during the trials, the Speaker removes Papagena: "Away with you, young woman, he is not yet worthy of you!" Nor is Tamino worthy of Pamina, for all her moral frailty, until he has been purified. Once that has happened, the male principle takes command. Tamino and Pamina both appear in the last scene dressed in priestly robes. As the devotees of the sun and its masculine power, the priests themselves have the final word. They invoke what every male wants for himself, that without which he cannot dominate, when they sing "Es siegte die Stärke und krönet zum Lohn"—"the strong have conquered and may they be crowned with praise."[15]

In reaching this culmination, Tamino and Pamina have traveled through the death of their underground initiation and been reborn to a higher being. The same thing happens to Belmonte and Constanze, who face death together in their heroic duet and then joyfully go on to live again. But getting what they want, the earlier lovers seem less inspiring than the Pasha who does not. For Belmonte and Constanze are only static characters. Unlike them, Tamino and Pamina change as they move through life. In the aria of the two Armed Men, we learn that life itself is a mystical journey, as the music (a Bach-like chorale set against a quasi fugue) suggests with its mood of pilgrims on their way. Tamino and

---

[15]These implications are somewhat lost in Ingmar Bergman's 1975 film version of *The Magic Flute.* By making Sarastro the affectionate father of Pamina and ending the opera with the young lovers dancing among courtiers who will recognize them as their legitimate rulers, Bergman eliminates the mystical symbolism that Mozart intended. Bergman presents the religious fable as a domestic drama about the transference of power from one generation to the next. That had been the theme of *Idomeneo,* the *opera seria* Mozart wrote just prior to *The Abduction;* but in *The Magic Flute* his mind was surely working in other directions.

Pamina follow this path beyond the comprehension of a Belmonte or Constanze. Instead of passion, they give themselves to a love that now goes by the name of Reason and Conjugality.

At the beginning of his mystical journey, Tamino travels in search of an image. He falls in love with Pamina merely by looking at her portrait. With the same "ich fühl' es" that she later uses for the pain of passion, he expresses the rapturous excitement that suddenly fills him. In the Da Ponte operas, Mozart had also associated love with images. In *Così*, Dorabella and Fiordiligi first appear to us in the act of admiring miniatures of their young men; in *Figaro*, Susanna begins her erotic explorations with a scene in which she tries on a new hat and beautifies herself while looking in the mirror; in *Don Giovanni*, the symbolism of love's imagery occurs in the constant use of masks that duplicate the human face while also falsifying it. In these operas images are always a way of playing with reality, and sometimes a substitute for it. One feels that the women in *Così* are so easily fooled by their boyfriends' disguises because they do not know what they really look like: they know them *only* through their images. By the end of the comedy, they have learned something and are better equipped to inspect the reality of their lovers. In *The Magic Flute*, however, Tamino's journey does not reveal a Pamina other than the one he originally encountered in the portrait. That was true and reliable, like their love itself. Instead of being a falsification, her image is but the first step in his progress into reality. To achieve his ends, he must purify his feelings and overcome the flaws in passion represented by the Queen of the Night. A comparable development occurs in Pamina. Together they clarify and perfect the passionate, subduing it for the needs of a rationalized marriage.

Writing about Mozart as a dramatist, Brigid Brophy tries to prove that *The Magic Flute* consists of two plots superimposed upon one another, the earlier having been changed for reasons of Masonic secrecy.[16] To Terrasson's *Life of Sethos*, from which the libretto was originally drawn, she thinks that Mozart later added

[16]For an exhaustive analysis of the Masonic symbolism in the opera, see Jacques Chailley, *The Magic Flute: Masonic Opera* (New York: A. A. Knopf, 1971). See also Paul Nettl, *Mozart and Masonry* (New York: Philosophical Library, 1957), and the chapters on *The Magic Flute* in Dent, *Mozart's Operas*. For this and other aspects of *The Magic Flute*, see Maurice Kufferath, *La Flûte Enchantée de Mozart* (Paris: Librairie Fischbacher, 1914–19), and Alfons Rosenberg, *Die Zauberflöte: Geschichte und Deutung von Mozarts Oper* (Munich: Prestel Verlag, 1964).

elements of the Orpheus myth. Whether or not Brophy's speculations are warranted, she is right in calling attention to the resemblance between Tamino and Orpheus. Tamino is an inspired musician; his flute can tame the wild beasts just as Orpheus's lyre could. In *The Magic Flute* the beasts appear almost gratuitously and then disappear after a musical interval that seems to have nothing to do with the plot. Actually, this little scene illustrates the meaning and the efficacy of the magic flute. Since the flute signifies man's power to control human passions, the wild animals (like Monostatos, whose black heart makes him a suitable ally for the Queen of the Night) symbolize the savagery of all sexual emotions. When Socrates asks the aged Cephalus in Plato's *Republic* how he feels about losing libidinal drive as old men do, Cephalus replies that it is like being freed from subjugation to a raging beast. In various primitive cultures, the flute was thought to have magical powers for purifying bodily impulses as well as regenerating them. The sacred flutes could effect sexual potency, harmony in love, and rebirth after death. Among the Iatmul of the Pacific, flutes belonged to a male cult in which a monster—like the one that pursues Tamino at the beginning of the opera—chases all the women but finally does no harm to anyone.[17]

In using the magic flute to tame and purify the passions, Tamino achieves the ability to return from death hand in hand with his beloved. Sexual intercourse—*la petite mort,* as the French call it—has often been represented as a descent into death. Through it, lovers lose their separate lives and unite in an unknown adventure that ends in a blurring of consciousness. Sarastro—whom the Queen of the Night calls an evil spirit—carries off Pamina just as Pluto, the god of death, had carried off Eurydice, the beloved of Orpheus. But as the Freemasons believe that death is nothing fearful, Sarastro turns out to be good and even holy. He tests the lovers, but he does not impede their return to life. If they can pass through the fire and water of sexuality, they

[17]See Donald E. Carr, *The Sexes* (New York: Doubleday, 1970), pp. 111–12. On the Iatmul and sacred flutes, see Margaret Mead, *Male and Female* (New York: Dell, 1968). See also Curt Sachs, *The History of Musical Instruments* (New York: W. W. Norton, 1940), pp. 45ff.; and Duncan MacDougald, Jr., "Music and Sex," *Encyclopedia of Sexual Behavior* (New York: Hawthorn Books, 1963), II, 747. On dragons as symbolic of "darkness, night and death" as well as the idea of emergence from waters as a slaying of dragons that represents the entrance into sacred reality, see Mircea Eliade, *The Sacred and the Profane: The Nature of Religion* (New York: Harcourt, Brace, & World, 1959), pp. 48, 130.

are worthy of everlasting oneness. In the course of his trial, Tamino must not talk to Pamina, just as Orpheus was not to look at Eurydice. Orpheus looked back, and therefore lost his spouse to the bondage of death. Unlike him, Tamino does not turn back—i.e. submit—to the female. He retains his dominance and finally helps Pamina liberate herself from the influence of her hateful mother.[18]

There are two ideals that govern the music and the action of this opera. One is the sacred love that binds Tamino to Pamina, as symbolized by the golden flute; the other is friendship, the love of mankind, that changes enmity into enduring peace and is symbolized by Papageno's silver bells. As Tamino tames the wild beasts with his flute, Papageno chimes Monostatos and the slaves into a melodious trance which Papageno and Pamina call "friendship's harmony." Gold ranking higher than silver, mystical love is given precedence over humanitarian friendship. Throughout the opera the former expresses itself through religious music while the latter relies upon folk music. But the principles interweave and presuppose each other. Papageno gets someone to love, just as Tamino finds permanent companionship in Pamina. Both ideals involve a kind of reason that supervenes upon sexuality and controls it in all its manifestations.

Exactly what this means, we never learn. For in being a fable, the opera avoids empirical or realistic details that might detract from the sublimity of its ideals. Women are to be ruled by men; and both the sensuous and the passionate are to be subordinated to the dictates of reason. Where this happens under the aspect of love and friendship, there results a conjugal union that resolves all human problems. Not through Christian devotion, but only in an acceptance of their own nature, can man and wife approximate that godhead of which Pamina and Papageno sing in their duet about love. And it can only be done on earth, within that haven of wholesome, conscientious living that Sarastro's temple represents. As he approaches it for the first time, Tamino says: "The doors and gates impart, / It is the home of Prudence, Work, and Art; / Where labor rules and force withdraws, / Vice cannot prevail."

This temple is the sanctuary that Beethoven sought all his life. Mozart brings us up to it, and then departs. *The Magic Flute* completes his vision of the world. As he lay dying, he lamented the

---

[18]For a somewhat different interpretation of turning back, and in general the idea of "zurück" in this opera, cf. Angus Fletcher, "On Two Words in the Libretto of *The Magic Flute*," *The Georgia Review*, Spring 1975.

fact—as if this mattered most to him—that now he would never see it performed again.

4. A Change of Perspective

In his *Life of Rossini,* Stendhal makes the following remark: "Mozart's unique position in the world of art is due precisely to his combination of these two dissimilar qualities, dramatic power and gentle sensuality; Michaelangelo is never anything but overwhelmingly powerful; Correggio is never anything but sweetly voluptuous."[19]

Assuming that Stendhal is right in what he says about Mozart, one must still ask whether a combination of the sensuous and the dramatic truly yields the passionate. Though he often and beautifully expresses the voice of passion, Mozart tends to distrust it more and more as he gets older. *Idomeneo,* his first great opera, contains a good deal of his most impassioned music. In it Ilia and Electra are both passionate women. The hostility between them, in many ways similar to the conflict between Aïda and Amneris, is a dramatic struggle between different types of passionate love. While Electra reveals the irrationality of passion, Ilia resembles Constanze in showing its craving for spiritual oneness. The operas Mozart wrote after *Idomeneo* and *The Abduction* depict alternative attitudes. In the Da Ponte operas, Electra reappears in the form of Elvira and Fiordiligi, but there are no women of the Ilia or Constanze type. In *The Magic Flute,* the differences between Ilia and Electra are duplicated by the contrast between Pamina's passions and those of her mother. Now, however, both alike are subjugated by priestly sentiments that have no comparable importance in *Idomeneo,* despite its ritualistic aura. Even the killing of the respective monsters shows a significant change. In *Idomeneo,* it is the culminating feat of male heroism that sanctifies Idamante's preference for Ilia and her innocent passion as opposed to the insanity of Electra's. In *The Magic Flute,* Tamino is incapable of slaying the monster that pursues him through passion's nocturnal realm, and he attains his beloved only through acts of religious or mystical transcendence.[20]

[19]Trans. Richard N. Coe (London: John Calder, 1956), pp. 468–69.

[20]On *Idomeneo*'s influence upon the later Mozart operas, see János Liebner, *Mozart on the Stage* (New York: Praeger, 1972), pp. 41ff. For a brief but excellent discussion of passion in *Idomeneo,* as well as the relationship between that opera and Beethoven's *Fidelio,* see Rosen, *The Classical Style,* pp. 180–81.

In general, Mozart's later music seems to question the ultimate goodness of passion as a whole—to resist, restrain, minimize the value of those libidinal outbursts and lovesick yearnings that were to become so dominant in the nineteenth century, though already anticipated by Monteverdi, Purcell, Gluck, and others. Throughout the last Mozart operas, the passionate is treated as something to be rectified, as a problem and not a solution.

Romantic passion as it exists in the subsequent tradition requires two things that were foreign to Mozart: despair of one's own abilities and dissatisfaction with the actual world. Mozart was often defeated by society, as Don Giovanni is continually frustrated in his sexual exploits; but life in both of them remains forever irrepressible. It bounds off in all directions, renewing itself in the act of escape and further creativity. One often hears that music would spurt forth out of Mozart, effortlessly and with pure spontaneity. The sexual imagery is worth noting, and possibly it helps to explain why Mozart could not really despair of his own powers any more than Don Giovanni might. At the same time, neither of them uses his energy to change the world. They are satisfied with current reality in a way that Beethoven or Wagner or any number of troubled Romantics were not. Don Giovanni makes love with no ideal in mind. Love is not an ideal for him, and he searches for no ideal beloved. He is a revolutionary but he has no political goals, just a passion for the sensuous. Even Tamino, that pilgrim on the way to earthly paradise, scarcely indicates how others may actually follow him. Mozart believes in brotherhood and harmony between the sexes, but he does not write music to further the establishment of a social order in which these would be the moral determinants.

In this respect, *Fidelio* belongs to a different world from *The Magic Flute*—a more dynamic world and one that is ever restless, for it always reaches beyond itself. Mozart's world is more or less self-contained. His music is autotelic, just as sexual activity is for Don Giovanni. Each was to be justified by its own inherent pleasures. It is absurd to say, as de Rougemont does, that Don Giovanni incarnates "absolute moral nihilism."[21] But it is true that for him, as for Mozart, the mere passage of time offers so many opportunities for enjoyment that one need not consider more remote and problematic ideal possibilities. Lesser mortals, like ourselves, cannot tolerate such adherence to the immediately aesthetic. We need to be constantly reminded of ethical principles and social aspirations.

---

[21]De Rougemont, *Love Declared,* p. 115.

Like Masetto or Don Ottavio, we look for someone who can express our ideas of universal justice in large and unmistakable letters.

For this aspect of human nature, one must go beyond Mozart. The passionate love of freedom, interpreted as a state of dignity all men deserve rather than merely a condition of sensuous pleasure, is not his major theme. For Beethoven it becomes the basis of a new religion.

CHAPTER IV

Beethoven:
The Passion in *Fidelio*

[*Fidelio*] belongs to that powerful race of calumniated works
upon which are outpoured the most inconceivable prejudices,
and the most manifest falsehoods; but the vitality of which is so
intense that nothing can prevail against it. Like those vigorous
beeches, born amid rocks and ruins, which finish by splitting the
rocks and piercing the walls, and which rise at last, proud and
verdant, all the more solidly implanted on account of the obstacles they have had to overcome in order to emerge; whilst the
willows which grew without any trouble upon the river bank, fall
into its bed, and perish forgotten.

> Berlioz, *A Critical Study of Beethoven's Nine Symphonies*

By the glorification of woman's fidelity, [*Fidelio*] chimed with
the master's humanitarian dogma. Still that subject embraced so
much that is alien and unassimilable to music that, properly
speaking, only the great *Overture* to *Leonore* shows clearly what
Beethoven would have us understand by a *drama*. . . . Is not the
dramatic action of the opera *'Leonore'* an almost repulsive dilution of the drama presented in the Overture?

> Wagner, *Beethoven*

Of all my children, [*Fidelio*] is the one that cost me the worst
birth-pangs, the one that brought me the most sorrow; and for
that reason it is the one most dear to me. Before all the others I
hold it worthy of being preserved and used for the science of
art.

     Beethoven, quoted in Romain Rolland, *Beethoven the Creator*

1. Beethovian Paradoxes

It is always hazardous to read a composer's personality in his
music; but Beethoven seems to encourage us in that direction more
than any other artist. The philosophical music critic may see in
Bach a baroque embellishment of Lutheran faith, in Handel a
quasi-mystical love of orderliness and grand decorum, in Mozart
that combination of "dramatic power and gentle sensuality" to
which Stendhal refers, and so on. Beethoven's music lends itself to
comparable generalizations, but also it reveals *Beethoven as a person*
in a way that no previous music had ever done. The subject in his
works includes the composer himself: his struggles, his problems,
his life as both a man and a creative spirit. It is fitting, therefore,
that Beethoven becomes the symbol of *all* artists in the last two
centuries. His scowling visage, whether on porcelain busts or teenage sweatshirts, shows not only the genius at work but also the
self-expression the modern world expects to find in the work of a
genius.

    The self that Beethoven expresses is, moreover, the self of one
who believes passionately in self-expression. Nietzsche said that "by
music the passions delight in themselves." But Beethoven's music
also generates the very passions it delights in expressing. In
some respects, they are more remote from mere sexuality than they
often were in Mozart. In his notebooks, Beethoven wrote: "Sensual
enjoyment without the union of souls is and always will be bestial;
after it there is no trace of an exalted sentiment, rather one feels
remorse."[1] We need only recall Mozart's letters to his wife—playful,
salacious, earthy, and innocent all at once—to see how different
was the moral and aesthetic development of these two men.

    Beethovian passion appears most explicitly in *Fidelio*. Though
Beethoven did not write the libretto, itself derived from a play by

---

[1]*Beethoven: Letters, Journals and Conversations*, p. 150.

Bouilly, he chose it out of countless texts that had been offered to him. Throughout his life he worked on overtures and incidental music to various dramatic vehicles, but he never wrote another opera. *Léonore ou l'amour conjugal* had been the original title; and in Bouilly, as in the musical versions of Gaveaux and Paër, the story of Leonore's heroism served to illustrate the beauty of conjugal love. But in Beethoven the story and its moral edification became secondary. The music dominates throughout, the orchestral design overwhelming the singers on occasion. Far from serving as the illustration of anything, the work becomes the tonal *embodiment* of the abstract concepts to which it is devoted. In an anecdote that Berlioz recounts, Beethoven is said to have told Paër: "I like your opera. I think I will set it to music."[2] Though Beethoven may never have said anything of the sort, his opera gives the ideas of heroism and conjugal love a significance they can have only in *his* kind of music. It is music that subordinates everything else to the expression of passion, music that expresses passions which belong to the composer's own passionate nature.

At the same time *Fidelio* is also a religious drama, as I shall try to show. The opera is a mystic rite by which Beethoven enunciates the spiritual aspirations of a revolutionary creed. *Fidelio* is the passion according to Beethoven—in both senses of the word *passion*. I shall first consider the nature of Beethoven's personal passion and then its sacramental function in his opera.

Once we approach the soul of Beethoven in *Fidelio*, we quickly come upon a series of paradoxes. Beethoven lived and spoke like a misanthrope; yet the opera idealizes the love of humanity. He never married and never seems to have enjoyed sexual love for any protracted period; yet the opera idealizes marital devotion.[3] He

---

[2]See "Fidelio" in Hector Berlioz, *A Critical Study of Beethoven's Nine Symphonies* (New York: Charles Scribner's Sons, 1913). On the unreliability of the anecdote, see Edward J. Dent's introduction to his translation of *Fidelio* (London: Oxford University Press, 1938), pp. xii–xiii. Paër's version is described in Winton Dean, "Beethoven and Opera," in *The Beethoven Reader*, ed. Denis Arnold and Nigel Fortune (New York: W. W. Norton, 1971), pp. 345–48. This chapter also includes useful analyses of the three versions of Beethoven's *Fidelio* (1805, 1806, and 1814). On the development of *Fidelio* throughout these versions, see Alexander Wheelock Thayer's *Life of Beethoven*, rev. and ed. Elliot Forbes (Princeton: Princeton University Press, 1967), pp. 346–47, 399–400, 576–88, and Irving Kolodin, *The Interior Beethoven: A Biography of the Music* (New York: A. A. Knopf, 1975), pp. 188–208. See also the *Fidelio* entry in Paul Nettl, *Beethoven Encyclopedia* (New York: Philosophical Library, 1956).

[3]For the (ambiguous and inconclusive) evidence about Beethoven's love-life, see George R. Marek, *Beethoven: Biography of a Genius* (New York: Thomas Y. Crowell, 1972), pp. 219–315.

continually labored under the charge of being tyrannical with the women he knew; yet the opera idealizes the courage of a Leonore who shows her love through action rather than submissiveness. Was Beethoven using the work to compensate for inadequacies in himself? Or was he demonstrating how pitifully the world fell short of what it ought to be? In his funeral oration, Grillparzer said of Beethoven: "He remained solitary because he could find no second I." Was this because of deficiencies in Beethoven, or in the rest of mankind?

I shall not try to answer these questions, but I think it is useful to examine a typical Freudian attempt to do so. In their study of Beethoven and his nephew, the Sterbas say the following about *Fidelio:* "Leonore, after whom the opera was originally named, since she plays the principal role, appears throughout the opera in male attire; she triumphs by her courage and daring; she rescues Florestan and brings him from the darkness of the deepest dungeon to the light of day. It is unmistakable that, years later, when he saved his nephew from destruction by the evil principle—Johanna [the boy's mother]—Ludwig assumed the role of Leonore himself. And in doing so, he too was a woman in man's clothing."[4] As evidence that Beethoven's masculine sexuality was transformed into a maternal love of his nephew, the Sterbas quote from an account of something Beethoven said in later life: "He said that he had never known of a marriage in which, after a time, one or the other partner had not regretted the step, and that, of the few young ladies whom he had in earlier days wished to make his own, considering that the height of happiness, he had later remarked to himself that he was very lucky that none of them had become his wife, and what a good thing it was that the wishes of mortals often remain unfulfilled."

This way of approaching Beethoven seems to me wholly erroneous. The statement about marriage does not signify that Beethoven's love for his nephew had destroyed his interest in women; and neither does it suggest that Beethoven was himself a woman in man's clothing, or that he secretly identified with Leonore. These cynical or pessimistic remarks of Beethoven do indicate an ambivalence that is worth exploring. But it is more complex than the Sterbas recognize, and it can more readily be understood by tracing the aesthetic function of Beethoven's idealizations in a

---

[4]Editha Sterba and Richard Sterba, *Beethoven and His Nephew: A Psychoanalytical Study of Their Relationship* (New York: Schocken Books, 1971), p. 111.

work like *Fidelio* than by speculating about details of his unconscious which are not likely to reveal themselves after all these years of deepening obscurity.

For similar reasons, I tend to distrust other psychiatrists who reduce Beethoven's art to some underlying schizoid or psychotic condition. Notice the language that Anthony Storr uses: "In compensation for his disappointment with, and resentment of actual human beings, Beethoven imagined an ideal world of love and friendship. . . . His music, perhaps more obviously than that of any other composer, displays considerable aggression in the sense of power, forcefulness, and strength. It is easy to imagine that, had he not been able to sublimate his hostility in his music, he might well have succumbed to a paranoid psychosis."[5]

In criticizing this passage, Rollo May argues that Beethoven's "schizoid state" must have been a very constructive means for dealing with his problems or else it could not have eventuated in great music.[6] Both Storr and May assume that Beethoven's work is an escape from dangers of pathology; and this is true in the trivial sense that without his music Beethoven *might* have been just another schizoid. But then, without his music Beethoven would have had less reason or capacity to cut himself off from other people. He would not have been the Beethoven we know, and possibly not a schizoid at all. He might have been just a boisterous bourgeois, which he also was. In any event, the reductivist approach tells us very little about Beethoven's creativity. For even if his music sublimates hostile emotions, it does so by expressing them in a work of art. The ideal world of love and friendship that Beethoven imagined is more than just the compensation for resentment and disappointment. It is also a human possibility that transcends the actual world, and the artist's need to delineate it for himself is as sane or healthy-minded as any other successful manipulation of reality. I doubt that we can understand the paradoxes in someone like Beethoven if we treat him like a paranoid psychotic *manqué;* but we may be able to elucidate his unique personality by studying the nature of his artistic idealizations.

When we concentrate upon *Fidelio* itself, we are immediately struck by the fact that Leonore is not a woman but a superwoman. She is a heroine of a sort that Pamina in *The Magic Flute* was not. Pamina is an ordinary damsel in distress, beautiful, good-hearted,

[5]Anthony Storr, *Human Aggression* (New York: Bantam Books, 1970), p. 99.
[6]Rollo May, *Love and Will* (New York: Delta Books, 1973), p. 17.

and courageous within the limits of her feminine capability. Leonore also shows the conventional female frailty, and after her confrontation with Pizarro in the second act she all but faints away. But
unlike Pamina, she is always an active agent, an originator of action.
She takes arms against a sea of troubles; she chooses her destiny as
a liberator; and in her transvestite disguise she behaves like the
traditional male hero who seeks to free his beloved from imprisonment. Leonore reverses the sexual stereotypes, defies the fate
that decrees the death of her husband, and yet remains a loving
woman throughout. It is clearly the image of a feminine hero, an
heroic female, that intrigues Beethoven.

In a notebook for the year 1818, when he was already 48 years
old, Beethoven wrote: "Only love, yes, only love is capable of grant-
ing you a happy life. O God, let me find her at last, the woman who
may strengthen me in virtue, who is permitted to be mine."[7] Is it
Leonore that Beethoven still hopes to find? If so, it is not surprising
that he never married. Ideals have a way of never appearing on
earth. If they did, they would be a new reality from which a Beethoven would always flee by creating some new ideal—a new Leonore, different from the first one but no less of an idealization.
Think of the line I quoted earlier: "What a good thing it was that
the wishes of mortals often remain unfulfilled." This makes sense if
one has a need and even a passion for idealization, and possibly
ideals are made to be elusive for the sake of generating passions
that someone like Beethoven can recreate through fictional beings
such as Leonore.

Being an idealization of this sort, Leonore is in principle a
distant beloved. She is *die ferne Geliebte,* as in Beethoven's song cycle.
In the distance, Novalis said, everything becomes poetic and
romantic. Leonore is constructed in the dimensions not of any
actual woman but of a remote possibility that stimulates the imagination, and so leads the creator to his own deeds of heroism
through creativity alone. She is often associated with Goethe's *ewige
Weibliche,* but that is inaccurate. For in the context of the opera,
Leonore appears less as a spiritual lure than as a will to action. She
is the figure of Liberty that Delacroix portrays on the barricades,
her magnanimous bosom bared as she holds aloft the flag of
humanistic revolution.

At the same time, one misconstrues Beethoven's humanitarian-
ism if one fails to recognize that this too was an ideal he could

---

[7]*Beethoven: Letters, Journals and Conversations,* p. 161.

hardly tolerate in reality. I am not thinking of his reputation as a domestic despot, nor of his ill-tempered statements about the pettiness of the human race. I am thinking rather of the airy abstractness in Beethoven's references to that Humanity which he claimed to love and for which he was writing his heroic music. Molière's Alceste, and indeed every misanthrope, can justify his hatred of men by claiming a superior and unrequited love of mankind. On that desert island to which Alceste exiles himself, what else would he do but write an opera like *Fidelio* or choral music like the last movement of the Ninth Symphony, glorifying humanity as it may someday be, provided that he does not have to endure it in its present imperfection?

The critic Paul Bekker put the matter quite precisely when he said: "What interested Beethoven was not the personal, the human, the sum of small characteristics which form an individual but the idea incarnate in some heroic figure."[8] But other than individual people—each of whom is small, human, and personal—what constitutes "humanity"? The idea incarnate in some heroic figure is only an idea, a fiction, a dramatic fantasy. It indicates a possible direction for moral endeavor; but in itself it is not a present reality in the sense in which people that one loves or hates are real and present. One marvels at its ability to supplant actual men and women in Beethoven's imagination.

In saying this, I am not suggesting that Beethoven's attitude was undesirable, or that he is deficient as a creative artist. It is often said that since Beethoven lacked Mozart's interest in people, the music of *Fidelio* cannot delineate persons with the insight, the subtlety, or the pointillistic genius of Mozart. I think this is true, but very misleading. For Beethoven uses a different brush-stroke, one that is broader and more monumental than anything Mozart could imagine; and he does so because he has a vision of humanity that Mozart never approximates. Though Mozart wrote hymns to mankind in the pious chords of his masonic faith, he has little conception of the human race as a whole. For him it is merely an empirical summation of those many individuals he understood and possibly loved. For Beethoven all humanity is one, a single entity with a single nature that no class of individuals could duplicate. It therefore requires a different devotion from the small-scale affection this or that person might engender. In Mozart one scarcely feels

[8]Quoted in W. J. Turner, *Beethoven: The Search for Reality* (London: Ernest Benn, 1927), p. 243.

the influence of Kant. In Beethoven his moral imperatives appear all the time. And perhaps it is *only* a misanthrope—or at least, a solitary sufferer—who can fully appreciate Kant when he says that "in all men we must honor the dignity of the whole race," and then defines dignity in relation to reason alone.[9] A Mozart would instinctively turn away from a philosopher who subordinates the variable sentiments of real people to an abstract and uniform dignity of the race. Beethoven finds the idea uplifting and inspiring. It enabled him to see human beings as the exemplar of something further. Possibly it convinced him that great art always treats people as more than merely particular persons.

Beethoven also differs from Mozart in his attitude towards political action. Among the Mozart operas we have considered there are heroic figures only in *The Abduction, The Magic Flute,* and *Idomeneo.* And in these the hero is a prince who wins a princess, as he would in any folk tale. But neither Belmonte nor Tamino has any political awareness, and Idamante fights the sea-monster with no realization that his purity of heart will have earned him the right to displace his father as king. The heroism in Mozart operas is always of the personal sort that medieval legends exploit. Even *Figaro,* for all its revolutionary intrigue, subordinates politics to the individual search for pleasure. In *Fidelio,* however, the female hero acts in a way that liberates a man who is not only her husband but also a heroic liberator himself. Her motivation is political as well as personal, and through her ability to use personal devices in a political cause (while also using political devices in a personal cause) she explores a region of female consciousness that Mozart knew nothing about. Plato, who with Kant was one of the few philosophers Beethoven read, believed that an ideal Republic would employ music to mold the passions of ordinary citizens in ways that could be politically beneficial. Napoleon thought the same. In one of his first letters as a consul, he wrote: "Among all the fine arts, music is the one which exercises the greatest influences upon the passions and is the one which the legislator should most encourage." The tone of such a remark is foreign to Mozart. It fits Beethoven's music perfectly—*Fidelio* as well as the Eroica Symphony, *Egmont* as well as the Ninth.

Even so, this political concern was still an idealization for Beethoven. Consider his angry statement when he took Napoleon's

---

[9]Cf. also Kant's ideas about marriage and sexuality in the *Lectures on Ethics.* Their similarities to the concept of love in *Fidelio* are worth exploring.

name off the title page of the Eroica. Having just learned that Napoleon now calls himself Emperor, Beethoven concludes that he cannot be the great liberator the world awaited: "Then he, too, is nothing but an ordinary man! Now he also will tread all human rights underfoot, will gratify only his own ambition, will raise himself up above all others, and become a tyrant."[10] As a prediction, these words turned out to be all too true—but possibly because Napoleon was not *enough* of an ordinary man. Like Beethoven himself, he was driven by an image of heroic achievement that stirs the soul but rarely conduces to the creation of a good society. The great leader may be inspired by passionate ambitions, but he acts in concrete ways that satisfy the moment-by-moment necessities of men and women. This side of political action Beethoven did not understand. He is a revolutionary only in feeling the upsurge of emotion afforded by the sheer *possibility* of amelioration in the human condition. The breaking of eggs in the hope of making omelets he could well appreciate; but the tedious work of cookery, the part of political action that consists in the making of the omelet, had no place in his imagination.

For this reason, men of action will always find Beethoven's music ultimately unsatisfying. He intrigues them by seeming to understand their moral cravings. But then, at the moment of political truth, his soul takes flight. Maxim Gorky quotes Lenin as saying of the *Appassionata:* "I would like to listen to it every day. It is marvelous, superhuman music. I always think with pride—perhaps it is naïve of me—what marvelous things human beings can do!" To this Lenin adds, not mentioning Beethoven's music but obviously thinking of it: "But I can't listen to music too often. It affects your nerves, makes you want to say stupid, nice things, and stroke the heads of people who could create such beauty while living in this vile hell. And now you mustn't stroke anyone's head—you might get your hand bitten off. You have to hit them on the head, without any mercy, although our ideal is not to use force against anyone. H'm, h'm, our duty is infernally hard."[11]

In the nineteenth-century culture to which Lenin was reared, it was precisely Beethoven's ability to affect one's nerves that was most highly prized. The forcefulness, and even violence, of his music provided an aesthetic substitute for hitting people on the

[10]*Beethoven: Letters, Journals and Conversations,* p. 30.
[11]Maxim Gorky, *Days with Lenin* (New York: International Publishers, 1932), p. 52.

head. So many years before Lenin, Beethoven too had said: "Our age requires strong-minded men who will flog these petty, treacherous, miserable scoundrels of human beings." Yet nothing but the drama of action enters into his work, nothing but the passion of politics. And perhaps that is why Tolstoy felt so great a revulsion towards Beethoven's music. In *The Kreutzer Sonata* his protagonist says: "Under the influence of such music it seems to me that I feel what I do not really feel, that I understand what I do not understand, that I can do what I cannot do." Tolstoy was revolted by the mere phenomenon of passion, with all its subterranean links to sexuality; but also he knew that even the noblest of political passions have no reliable consequences in moral action.

Here again, I am not suggesting that Beethoven failed in any way. I only point out that his music is both political by nature and also an idealization of emotions which do not necessarily lead to changes in human behavior or social institutions. In the Eroica Symphony, in the Fifth, in *Fidelio*—and in most of the music of Beethoven's early maturity—one senses a powerful will demanding a better world for human beings as a whole; one senses an angry rejection of artificial or tyrannical restraints upon man's freedom; one senses a passionate voice unsatisfied with petty compromises. But does one sense an actuality that would bring happiness or peace to this perturbed spirit? Occasionally, but not very often. In *Fidelio* there is a happy ending; but one can hardly envisage the stable married life of Florestan and Leonore. Liberty and the joy of marital bliss are each presented as eternal essences that must not be questioned too closely. They are the goals of a longing that may never be satisfied, and may never want to be.

As if with Beethoven in mind, Schopenhauer said that music differs from other arts inasmuch as "it is not an image of phenomena, or more correctly, of the adequate objectivity of the will, but an immediate image of the will itself, and represents accordingly the metaphysics of all that is physical in the world, the thing *per se*, which lies beyond all appearance."[12] Written in 1818, this remark can have no reference to the later Beethoven. But it suits the Beethoven of *Fidelio* very well. In that work, and in others of the same period, Beethoven expresses the being of a passionate will that seems to be demanding something no experience could possibly afford. As the conversations with Bettina Brentano indi-

---

[12]*The World as Will and Representation*, I, no. 52. Cf. also the reference to Beethoven in II, chap. 39.

cate, Beethoven thought that his music revealed the nature of ultimate reality.[13] His belief was an act of faith, and therefore beyond any profitable criticism. What matters most is the fact that so much of his work expresses unrelenting will, insatiable passion. If his music reveals an ultimate reality, it must be related to that condition, and to the likelihood that only in a work of art can such passion be enjoyed or fully consummated.

That Beethoven should have written the greatest opera about conjugal love while never finding it for himself is thus not a paradox after all. For he writes about the striving and not the achievement, about a will that can never terminate in experience, about a passion that cannot be consummated except in the artistic expression of passion. And possibly Beethoven could not have written about conjugal love at all if he himself had undergone the confusing complexities of the real thing.

2. *Fidelio* as a Mystic Rite

In being a dramatization of passion, of heroism, and of that aggressive wilfulness without which there could be neither passion nor heroism, *Fidelio* takes the form of a religious mystery. It is a passion play for that new religion of man which the French Revolution sought to establish and nineteenth-century romanticism nearly did. Like all mysteries, it presupposes a dualistic approach to human experience. There is the world above ground in which the opera begins; and there is the dungeon, below ground, the hidden being in which the holy performance completes itself. In earlier versions of *Fidelio,* Beethoven concluded his opera with the moment of victory in the dungeon. This accentuates the dualism. In its final form, however, the work ends above ground. This does not destroy the basic dualism; it merely unites the elements of reality at that level on which ordinary life exists. Speaking of a "metaphysical design" behind the musical plan, Marion Scott says:

> Each act opens simply, with few characters, then gradually gathers its forces until it expands into a broad concerted finale. But while Act I begins in bright daylight and banter with the simplicity of little everyday affairs and moves from them steadily

[13]For the context as well as the content of Beethoven's remarks, see Romain Rolland, *Goethe and Beethoven* (New York: Harper & Brothers, 1931). See also J. W. N. Sullivan, *Beethoven: His Spiritual Development* (New York: Vintage Books, 1960).

downward into the shadows of tragedy and the sighing of all that are desolate and oppressed in the prisoners' choruses, Act II begins below the threshold of hope, and from the lowest prison of the human soul in loneliness, as typified in Florestan, passes gradually upward to faith fulfilled in a burst of light more glorious than any sunrise.[14]

In ordinary life we are not aware of the two levels, and so Beethoven magnifies, enlarges each beyond its normal size. Though the prison is a grave, as the prisoners tell us, Beethoven presents it with the Baroque grandeur of a Piranesi print. In one of his studies of prison architecture, Piranesi sketches a gigantic man outstretched in suffering—reminiscent of Michelangelo's Adam but writhing like an antecedent of Florestan. In another, he casts two solitary figures, guards conversing with one another. They are dwarfed by the dimensions of their institution; but also its lines and mammoth spaces bestow a terrible importance upon their conversation. In Beethoven, too, the little problems of the jailer's family seem more momentous than if the scene were set in the local square. The awkwardness of Jaquino, a latter-day Masetto; the fickleness of Marzelline; the paternal solicitude of Rocco—all this is bourgeois comedy. And yet, it immediately issues into the bizarre contrivance of a Leonore so well disguised that Marzelline can fall in love with her. Village love is not that blind; and even if it were, it could hardly deceive Rocco as well. We easily suspend disbelief, however, because we are intimidated by the awesomeness of Beethoven's prison. We also know that traditionally heroism is a masculine trait. If Leonore is to be an heroic female in the myth, she may very well appear under the guise of a wandering bachelor. Jaquino stutters his proposal of marriage to music that is almost mocking in its hesitation: "Ich—ich habe—ich habe...." Though she does not know who or what Fidelio is, Marzelline prefers him as any girl would naturally choose a knight rather than a squire. Without realizing it, she is in love with the heroic mission that has led him to this grim, unlikely spot.

Thus even at the level of the bourgeois and the commonplace, we are already in the realm of myth. All the details of the opera are controlled by the necessity of having the female hero descend into the lower reality. She cannot do this except as Rocco's companion, and she cannot become his companion except as his prospective

[14]Marion M. Scott, *Beethoven* (London: J. M. Dent & Sons, 1937), pp. 198-99.

son-in-law. The plot arranges this, intriguing us with the difficulties of sexual miscegenation. As a way of organizing the confusion, the music issues into a quartet that expresses the varying attitudes of Leonore, Marzelline, Rocco, and Jaquino while also presenting them in a canon that suggests an underlying unity. In fact, the oneness of the canonic form dominates the *Mir ist so wunderbar* quartet to such an extent that all divergency in sentiment seems wholly incidental. Although the four characters have conflicting points of view, Beethoven accords them very little musical differentiation. Instead they are merged into an exalted and quasi-religious *sostenuto* that transcends their individual interests.[15] Unlike Verdi in the *Rigoletto* quartet, Beethoven cares less about dramatic characterization than about the single mythic purpose for the sake of which these characters have been created.

Exactly *what* that is, the quartet does not tell us. We see the goal that unites these voices only after Rocco sings (in solid and easily negotiable music) his paean to money as the basis of a sound marriage. As against this idea, Leonore replies that only "the union of two kindred hearts" can assure marital bliss. Since Florestan languishes in the dungeon, she must descend to prove that Rocco's view is wrong even for the superficial world. Her heroic oneness with Florestan unifies both levels of reality. It is the end, the telos, of every moment in both the drama and the music.

In her book on Mozart, Brigid Brophy suggests that Leonore is an extension of Pamina, herself a development of Constanze in *The Abduction*. The name "Fidelio" is a synonym of "Constanze"; Belmonte calls Constanze "Engels Seele!" just as Florestan has a vision of "Ein Engel, Leonoren"; and the final duet between Constanze and Belmonte is "a concentrated sketch of what Beethoven was to expand into *Fidelio*, namely the identity of husband and wife."[16] At the same time, Miss Brophy sees that Constanze is too passive to prefigure Leonore. In her opinion, Pamina does so when she turns into an "active principle without whose assistance Tamino could not have come successfully through his ordeals."[17]

While much of this is correct, the differences between Leonore and the Mozart heroines should not be minimized. Beethoven's opera is subtitled "the triumph of married love," but really it is

[15]On this, see Herbert F. Peyser, *"Fidelio,"* in *Introduction to Opera* (New York: Barnes & Noble, 1956), p. 89.

[16]Brophy, *Mozart the Dramatist*, p. 124.

[17]Ibid., p. 125. See also Edward J. Dent's introduction to *Fidelio*, p. xiv.

dedicated to *married love as a basis for action.* The trials of Constanze and Belmonte or of Pamina and Tamino are designed to prove that the lovers were made for each other. Leonore and Florestan are not being subjected to tests of that sort. They have already passed through the premarital fires that confront Mozart's characters. Instead of proving their oneness, they use it to work as a team; and what they work for becomes as important to the mythology of the opera as the fact that they love each other. Mozart's heroes and heroines have nothing in the world to do. Once they attain one another in a suitable marriage, they need only enjoy each other's presence forever after. Beethoven's protagonists devote themselves to the cause of human freedom—freedom for all people, in all places, and at all times. The opera portrays one episode in the endless struggle towards that ideal. And though there are moments of celebration, as in the finale, we are to assume that the lovers' passionate yearning—for each other as well as what they believe in—will also continue unendingly.

If Leonore is an angel in Florestan's vision, it is obvious that she is the angel of liberation, the harbinger of freedom. Indeed, Florestan identifies her as an angel who leads him "to freedom in the heavenly realm." In the *Vita Nuova* Dante had spoken of Beatrice as an emanation from God, an instance of divine agapē in the form of womanly beauty, an angel that walked the earth for a religious end not wholly different from the coming of Christ. Heretical as this idea undoubtedly was, it eluded censorship throughout the Middle Ages. A woman could symbolize Christ because each was holy through submissiveness and gentle forebearance. Before working on *Fidelio,* Beethoven had contemplated, but never written, an oratorio to be entitled *The Redeemer's Journey into Hell.* This is the trip that Leonore takes. But now the angelic female has a mission that is humanistic, and not especially Christian. It is simply the bringing of freedom, here and now if possible, and if not, then in that better place which Florestan calls heaven as a way of indicating its sheer ideality. Florestan's vision recurs in Egmont's dream of his sweetheart Klärchen dressed as "a Goddess of Liberty." She brings Egmont the laurel crown of a victor, though he is soon to be executed. Earlier Klärchen had sung about the "joy it would be to be changed to a man" who could serve as a soldier in Egmont's cause. She is a lesser Leonore, but still a woman of the same type.

In his soliloquy, Florestan does not realize that the angel of freedom is about to liberate him, but we have already seen her in operation on the upper level to which Act I is devoted. Searching for her husband, Leonore has succeeded in giving a moment's respite to the prisoners aboveground. They wander about dazed by this unexpected liberty but reverential in their appreciation. Beethoven expresses the holiness of freedom, of all and any freedom, by constructing the prisoners' chorus into a gradual crescendo of gratitude which always reminds me of Bellini's painting of St. Francis extending his arms to the sunshine and the open countryside outside his cave. More dramatically than *The Magic Flute,* and closer to the reality of human suffering, *Fidelio* contrasts the goodness of daylight with the fearfulness of the night, that darkness of the tomb to which the prisoners have become habituated. Freedom is the sun they seek; and though she cannot provide it permanently, Leonore acts like the angel of deliverance in allowing it into their lives for at least a little while. Beethoven shrewdly has the prisoners restrain their joy in Act I. Until Florestan is saved, the idea of freedom cannot assert itself in all its glory. The prisoners must return to their cells; Leonore must carry her light into the dungeon before they are finally liberated.

Leonore can effect the release of Florestan because he too has dedicated his life to deeds of liberation. He would not have been imprisoned in the first place except for his political heroism. In destroying a Florestan, Pizarro would be annihilating the cause of human freedom as well. When Don Fernando arrives as the actual liberator, he proclaims the ideals in which Florestan believed. He will not let the prisoners kneel slavishly. "The brother seeks his brother," he declares, "and if he can help, he gladly will." Only later does he learn that his courageous friend Florestan has been incarcerated here. Leonore herself manifests her husband's dedication when she promises to set free the unknown prisoner in the dungeon, whoever he may be, even if he is not Florestan. None of this existed in the original Bouilly play. In Beethoven's opera it is crucial.[18]

Not only does Leonore symbolize the cause of freedom, but also her activism leads the music in this opera as well as the plot. As sexual *libertà* dominates *Don Giovanni* to such an extent that even the masked avengers join the protagonist in singing to it, so does Leonore's mission force Pizarro to join her and the others in the moment of his own defeat. After the trumpet call has announced

[18]On the differences between the Bouilly play and the Beethoven opera, see Michael Levey, "Leonore and Fidelio," *Musical Times,* February 1961. See also Patrick J. Smith, *The Tenth Muse,* pp. 182–83.

the arrival of Don Fernando, the four principals of the opera sing together while Leonore's voice rings out above the rest. With a soaring emphasis upon *die Liebe,* she leads the frenzied quartet with the idea that love and courage shall set us free. She herself has been the trumpet call, the standard, the pillar of light that rises through the darkness. Pamina had said, "I lead you myself, and love guides me on," but we never really see her in action. Leonore shows us what Pamina had only suggested, her constant love leading humanity upwards into freedom.

But though she is heroic, Leonore is not a militant female. Like the heroines in Mozart, she assumes the aggressive role only reluctantly. She may guide the male to freedom, and she may assert herself against a tyrannical Pizarro, but she does not pretend to the kind of dominance that men have regularly taken for themselves in the western world.

Beethoven articulates this aspect of Leonore's character very carefully in the *Abscheulicher* aria. It has the three-part structure that was traditional for a classical soprano declamation, and Beethoven uses each of its elements to express ideas about female emotionality that are basic to the entire opera. As in the dramatic scena *Ah, perfido!* that Beethoven had written in his youth, the aria begins with an outburst of feminine indignation, which then turns into feelings of tenderness, and finally resolves itself as a kind of aggressiveness justified by an *innern Triebe,* a "spiritual impulse." In both arias, the elements contribute to a dialectic that suggests a thesis-antithesis-synthesis about the nature of woman. But where the heroine of *Ah, perfido!* modulates within the varieties of personal passion, like Donna Anna demanding vengeance, Leonore expresses a humanitarian purpose that eventuates in moral fervor suitable to the wife of a hero. Her initial anger turns into a sense of hope; and her final determination asserts itself in the name of a love that synthesizes everything else, a love that will not flinch or falter, an imperious instinct for conjugality, fierce and tender at the same time. Leonore may dress like a man, and she may have to brandish a pistol, but her hand quivers.[19] Far from wanting to dominate, she wishes to free her husband for the moral action that defines his being. The brasses, particularly the French horns, support her in this resolve, as if they were the voice of that virile but incapacitated man who needs his wife to help him in his labors.

Since she is not a masculine female, Leonore may be seen as

[19]As Berlioz writes, "I can still see Madame Devrient, stretching out her trembling arm in the direction of Pizarro" (*Beethoven's Nine Symphonies,* p. 153).

the mother who descends from the purity of some virgin state to give life and sustenance to her child, or even to hover protectively over his corpse, as in Michelangelo's *Pietà*. Though he is a hero in his own right, Florestan has also been reduced to a condition of dependency. Leonore feeds him in the dungeon and brings him into the world of daylight, much as a mother nourishes her infant in the dungeon of her womb but then liberates him through parturition. Leonore even strikes off his fetters, that umbilical cord which had bound him to his imprisonment. After his prolonged weakness, he then falls upon her breast.

As in the passage I previously quoted, one psychoanalytic interpretation finds in Leonore the effeminate and mothering side of Beethoven himself. Possibly there is *some* truth in this. Perhaps it even explains why Beethoven speaks of the opera as a child for whom he has suffered terrible "birth-pangs." But if we are to identify Beethoven with one or another of his characters, surely it is more plausible to identify him with Florestan. His first word— "Gott!"—resounds through the dungeon as a lengthy and supplicating cry to the principle of creativity that Beethoven worshipped throughout his life. It is the ritual utterance *aus der Tiefe,* from the depths, of the crushed but striving male. He is enclosed within his own destiny, as John Donne says: "We are all conceived in close Prison; in our Mothers' wombs, we are close Prisoners all; when we are borne, we are borne but to the liberty of the house; Prisoners still though within large walls."

Chained to the rock of this reality, Florestan reminds us of Prometheus in that early work of Beethoven's. Throughout his life, Beethoven thought of himself as a Promethean—a titan neither god nor man, but something in between who liberates mankind and suffers horribly for having done so. "Whoever understands my music will henceforth be free of the misery of the world," he is quoted as saying.[20] And possibly with Florestan's aria in mind, he remarks: "Words are bound in chains, but, happily, sounds are still free."[21] In *Prometheus and his Creatures* he had shown the divine fire of art bringing statues into life. In *Fidelio* the Promethean male is himself represented as a lifeless thing that must be warmed and eventually revitalized. Mozart's *Don Giovanni* had depicted a statue

[20]Quoted in Burnett James, *Beethoven and Human Destiny* (London: Phoenix House, 1960), p. 166.
[21]Quoted in Bishop Fan S. Noli, *Beethoven and the French Revolution* (New York: International Publishers, 1947), p. 84.

destroying life; and since the life of the sensuous male was nothing but immorality to Beethoven, he would surely have approved. It is only once the male becomes uplifted by a passionate search for humanitarian ideals that Beethoven will allow him to outdo the statue.

The darkness to which Florestan has been condemned may well symbolize the deafness that progressively isolated Beethoven from human affection.[22] If Florestan and Beethoven himself surmount their destiny, it is because neither ceases to struggle. This of course was to be the moral of Goethe's *Faust;* and it suitably applies to male pretensions throughout western culture. Despite the depression and misery with which Florestan's initial aria begins, it portrays him as a man who does not give up. Like the *Abscheulicher* aria, this one is also divided into three sections. But instead of a dialectical movement, its elements are organized into a linear progression—three steps upward, one after the other. First, there is a lament about imprisonment, ending with an acceptance of God's will. This leads into a more buoyant realization that Florestan has only done his duty. That turns into a final exaltation as he senses the approach of the redeeming angel—"ein Engel, Leonoren"—who will restore his freedom.

When Pizarro is about to kill him, Florestan takes another step upwards. As the orchestra surges heroically, he rises to a level of defiance in verbally attacking the aggressor who claims a right to vengeance. Thereafter, Leonore takes over. She guides the hero safely through the valley of the shadow of death. She has descended like Orpheus to save her beloved spouse. But unlike Orpheus, she does not waver or look back, and so Florestan lives again.

The mythic rebirth of Florestan, his return to life through his courage and the efforts of an angelic woman, depends on more than the married couple alone. It requires the godlike power of men like Don Fernando, the deus ex machina who actually effects the liberation. In him Beethoven had the opportunity of creating a new Sarastro. But he makes no such attempt. Don Fernando is less impressive, less awe-inspiring. Perhaps Beethoven had difficulty identifying with a political authority; perhaps he wished to subordinate all other ideals to the freedom-loving heroism of Leonore and Florestan. Nevertheless, he recognizes the utility of a Don

[22]On this, see Alan Tyson, "Beethoven's Heroic Phase," *Musical Times,* February 1969.

Fernando, as well as the importance of humble intermediaries like Rocco. As if he were Charon ferrying between life and death, Rocco descends with Leonore and returns with Florestan. But though he is a Charon-figure, Rocco also transcends his mythic function. For the association with noble creatures like Fidelio and Florestan seems to elevate his morality. When Pizarro offers him money—whose goodness Rocco has just been extolling—he refuses it rather than commit a murder. Under the humanizing influence of Leonore, he allows that momentary freedom to the prisoners and later comforts Florestan for the first time after all the months of systematic neglect. By the end of the opera, it is Rocco who speaks for the two heroes. At least, it is he who steps forward to inform Don Fernando of their identity and to condemn Pizarro.

Rocco mediates not only between the sunshine and the dungeon, between life and death, between freedom and enslavement, between the hardness of gold and the softness of his awakening sympathy, between the tyranny of a Pizarro whom he initially serves and the nobility of a Don Fernando to whom he eventually turns, but also—and most significantly—between suffering humanity and the constraints that society has imposed upon it. The chorus of prisoners in Act I resembles, or at least reminds us of, the chorus of priests in *The Magic Flute*. But though the music is equally reverential in both cases, it belongs to different religious attitudes. The prisoners attain a kind of holiness *simply* because they have suffered. Their music is sacred not only in celebrating the mystic qualities of the sun, as in Mozart, but also in arising from the souls of men who have been victimized by actuality. It does not matter that they may be criminals, or even murderers as hateful as Pizarro himself. They suffer, for whatever reason, and that makes them real and human to Beethoven in a way that never appears in Mozart's music. For Beethoven life is not a journey, as *The Magic Flute* maintained: it is a universal agony that only the greatest sympathy and the greatest dedication can overcome. No one, however vile, is to be excluded from the love that all men deserve. Beethoven even wanted Pizarro spared the punishment that the angry crowd demands in the final version of *Fidelio*. Originally, Leonore and Florestan interceded on Pizarro's behalf, convincing Don Fernando that Pizarro did not have the moral fortitude to undergo the suffering he himself had meted out, and therefore should be pardoned.

To have ended the opera that way—the tyrant restored to

human dignity along with Florestan—might have confused the moralistic audience, but it would have served Beethoven's inspiration perfectly. In being a human mystery, *Fidelio* has little to tell us about law or public policy or even penal reform. Retribution is too petty, and justice too much like bookkeeping, for its passionate aspirations. And anyhow, Pizarro is a man like any other. Though he is evil and must be defeated, it is his sheer humanity as one who errs that Beethoven cares about more than anything else. The words Pizarro utters in his first-act aria are fearful and diabolical—so much so that he sounds almost ridiculous to a twentieth century no longer living within the conventions of musical melodrama. But the orchestra that supports and interweaves the tyrant's voice is neither diabolical nor ridiculous. It is agitated and angry, but in a manner that could possibly have expressed the struggles of a moral hero. In short, it is the usual music for Beethovian passion. In all his perversity of motive, Pizarro too is furiously seeking some kind of freedom. We can infer that his kind is evil—indeed we must do so for the plot to make sense—but the orchestral texture presents his striving as just a bit of that transempirical will which underlies the dynamism of life in general. Only in Act II, when Pizarro physically confronts Florestan, does the orchestra recognize the fact that he is really evil. For now there is the dramatic possibility of his actually murdering the hero. Continuing the black and gloomy mood of the dungeon, the music becomes twisted, ugly, frightening. We now see the will in its most hideous aspect, as Faust does when he calls forth the earth-spirit. How can this be loved, even by an angel and her humanitarian husband?

Beethoven does not tell us. Pizarro is led away by soldiers, and we are expected to forget about him. Where Bouilly had an invisible chorus shouting "Vengeance! Vengeance!" Beethoven introduces the jubilant *Heil sei dem Tag.* Our attention is needed for the phenomenon of reconciliation among the victors: the lovers with each other, the prisoners with society. Since the will strives towards an elusive end beyond itself, it can never be fully satisfied. Still, it can sing the praises of those who keep on struggling. Perhaps that is why Beethoven revised the finale as he did. Instead of ending the opera soon after the joyful duet of the reunited couple in the dungeon, he goes on to the expansive music of thanksgiving to God and adulation of Leonore. The duet *O namen-namenlose Freude!* thus becomes a moment of private joy to balance the public celebration that follows in the next scene. And

137

certainly, something of the sort was needed. Otherwise, we could not have reached a contrasting oneness that embraces all humanity instead of two isolated individuals.

In his adoration of Mozart, Goethe tried to write a sequel to *The Magic Flute*. He never finished his libretto, though he used the material for the scenes in heaven of *Faust*, Part II. Where Goethe failed, Beethoven succeeded. The ending of *Fidelio* completes the mythology of *The Magic Flute*. There is no heaven here, but then there wasn't any for Mozart either. With Leonore's voice marching on before, rising above the rest as if to indicate an order of importance, the company thanks the God of righteousness who "tries us but does not forsake us." These are men and women on earth, yearning for a divinity that has touched them in their unexpected joy but still eludes their comprehension. The joyfulness of this music is reminiscent of the glorious finale to the second act of *The Abduction*. There, the lovers having found each other and Belmonte having assured himself that Constanze remained faithful in the harem, the orchestra and vocal quartet sing the praises of Love Triumphant. But Beethoven's jubilation is even grander. For he brings the entire commonwealth into his celebration. The real communion occurs among the people themselves. The massive choruses in the finale are not the heavenly choirs. They are the vehicles of mere humanity. When Leonore sings that it was through the power of love that she was able to free Florestan, she means the human love of human beings. With the requisite monumentality, the choruses and full orchestra passionately give their hearts to Leonore herself, praising her and reiterating the magnificence of her achievement. Over and over again, first the voices and then the orchestra call her "Retterin, Retterin"—the leader, the female knight, the saviour of her husband and of all mankind.

In the culminating clangor of the finale, the choruses sing with freedom and an open heart. For that is the meaning of human victory. Participating in the ritual, they have achieved the liberation that music itself provides. Don Fernando's amnesty brings more than just an escape from imprisonment. As members of the great chorus, the prisoners are liberated by virtue of their ability to glorify in sound the freedom and the holiness of human love. To this end, Beethoven introduced into the text a modified version of those words by Schiller that he was later to use again in the Ninth Symphony: "Wer ein holdes Weib errungen/ Stimm' in unsern Jubel ein!" Let him who has won a fair wife join in our rejoicing!

Leonore is that wife, but the music in both works merges her with something that goes beyond conjugality and is more than merely feminine. Through the harmony of an idealized marriage, the struggling will completes itself. And in doing so, it not only reconciles male and female but also those who are alienated from themselves and from their fellow men. It is a joyfulness that only those who have suffered can fully appreciate. It is the infinite goal of passion.

3. Gluck and Wagner

Beethoven's passionate idealizations appear more clearly when we contrast *Fidelio* with Gluck's *Alceste*. That opera is also devoted to conjugal love. In it Alcestis gives her own life in order to bring her husband Admetus back from the dead. Gluck's *Orfeo* employs a more graphic descent into the underworld, but *Orfeo* is a study in male rather than female mythology. *Alceste* is the real forerunner of *Fidelio*. More than any other great opera of the late eighteenth century, it provides Beethoven with a model of feminine devotion, examined in grandiose terms and with a happy ending that solves all problems.

At the same time, *Alceste* belongs to a wholly different ideology from *Fidelio*. For in it the female remains essentially submissive and dependent. Alcestis is primarily wife and mother, and she conducts herself like a member of the household rather than a social equal. The king on the level of ordinary life, and the infernal deities on the level of underlying reality, are male potentates who run the universe. The woman condemns herself to death because she believes that by her very nature she is inferior. Only in giving herself can she act as a woman should. She justifies her self-sacrifice by the fact that the world needs its masculine leader. Since he is her husband, it is quite normal for her to die as a means of keeping him alive.

As a result, there is little in Gluck's opera that actually *shows* the heroism of Alcestis. For a brief while in the first act she deliberates about the oracle's prediction—namely, that Admetus can survive his illness only if another dies for him. Realizing that she herself must make the requisite sacrifice, she courageously strengthens her resolve. In these moments Alcestis does appear like an heroic figure of the sort that Leonore is throughout *Fidelio*. But once Alcestis has chosen death, her passion takes a different direction: she becomes a *suffering* rather than an *active* heroine. The greatest pages in the opera include the music of mourning and regret, those long passages that reveal the grief occasioned by the death of Alcestis. Admetus cannot live without her, the children are pitiful in their loss, and the choruses bewail the disappearance of such a woman. Much of the opera deals with the actual dying of Alcestis. In fact, it is a study in female pathos. For all her nobility, the woman shows herself as a wounded, even masochistic, creature rather than the agency of moral and constructive change.

In part at least, all this results from the fact that Alcestis lives and dies for none of the humanitarian ideals that motivate Beethoven's heroine. Alcestis loves her husband; she is a dutiful wife and mother; and she is blessed in having her love acknowledged and reciprocated. She dies as a testament to her own devotion as well as to the worthiness of its object. But though her husband is the king, she hardly dies for a social or political end. In revising the myth as it originally appeared in Euripides, Gluck and his librettist Calzabigi concentrate upon wifely devotion as an isolated ideal. Within their classical setting, they limit themselves to a strain of personal emotion that even the romantic operas of the nineteenth century had to clothe in some pseudo-historical fiction.

In Euripides the drama deals with hospitality as a social ideal rather than conjugal love in a particular woman. The death of Alcestis precedes the action, which consists in Admetus's attempt to hide the painful truth from his guest Hercules. At the end, Hercules brings Alcestis back from the dead as a way of showing gratitude for the hospitality of Admetus. Nothing of this remains in Gluck's opera. In the Italian version, Hercules does not appear at all, Alcestis being restored by an Apollo who intervenes at the last moment as a purely mechanical deus ex machina. In the French version of the opera, Hercules contributes to the happy ending, but in a way that does not challenge the primacy of the wife's gesture.

Only in *Fidelio* are the social and personal merged as mutually supporting ideals. Euripidean hospitality turns into a love of humanity that matters to Leonore as much as to Florestan; and as Hercules was heroic in preventing the death of one who should live, so too is Leonore heroic not in dying for her husband but in bringing him back to life. The prevailing beauty of *Alceste* lies in the serenity of a woman who accepts her fate with a majesty that only Gluck's spacious music could convey. Admetus does not share this serenity. He rants and rails against destiny in ways that merely diminish him. Though he is active, he is not heroic. In *Fidelio* both husband and wife are heroes, and both take action against injurious fate. Their music is never sad, though sometimes gloomy; and if it lacks the serenity of submissiveness, it nevertheless moves us with the grandeur and the glory of moral dedication.

It is this achievement, I think, that Wagner sought to emulate in his heroic music dramas. The influence of *Fidelio* upon them was perfectly obvious to him. It was from Beethoven that he learned how sung melody might be integrated with the symphonic design for the sake of a more unified dramatic impact. So much was Wagner impressed by Beethoven's use of the orchestra in his vocal works that he felt they could even have dispensed with the words entirely. Speaking of the Ode to Joy in the Ninth Symphony, Wagner said: "It is not the sense of the words that takes hold of us when the human voice enters, but the *tone* of the human voice itself. Nor do the thoughts expressed in Schiller's verses occupy us hence-forth, but rather the cordial sound of choral singing. . . . It is quite evident that Schiller's words have only been made to fit the main melody as best they could."[23]

Doubtless what Wagner says is true in the sense that Beetho-ven's music far exceeds the banal words that were taken from Schiller. But if the tone of the human voice enables the music to have its effect upon us, that is largely due to the importance which Beethoven attached to the ideas that Schiller's words express. We must not be *distracted* by the thoughts of Schiller; but unless we feel them with a passion such as Beethoven's, we will not be able to appreciate the music as an occasion for emotional catharsis. One senses that, despite his radical protestations, Wagner simply did not believe this "humanitarian dogma" in the way that Beethoven and Schiller did.

Perhaps that also explains Wagner's notion that *Fidelio* is in-ferior to the Leonore Overture Number 3. Wagner would seem to think that the musical drama and all the vocal parts are dispens-able, or at least less interesting than the symphonic ideas expressed by this overture alone. In one respect, he is certainly right: Leonore Number 3 is more than just an introduction to an opera. It is also its metaphoric transformation into purely orchestral terms. Far from merely being a part of *Fidelio*, this overture stands to the opera as a correlative means of expressing similar attitudes. For that reason, I think conductors may be justified in performing Leonore Number 3 between the scenes of the second act, as Mottl and Mahler used to

---

[23]*Beethoven*, p. 70.

do, or even at the end of the entire opera.[24] Without being an intermezzo, the piece becomes a final restatement, a heightened and more comprehensive testimony to abstract heroism that need not be limited to the presence of people on a stage. To say this, however, is not to denigrate the opera itself, or to consider it a mere "dilution." Hearing Leonore Number 3 is no substitute for seeing *Fidelio*.[25]

But perhaps one should not take Wagner's criticism too literally. For it was from the ensembles and the choruses of *Fidelio* that he learned how to construct the vocal polyphony in *Lohengrin* and the second act of *Tannhäuser*. And where Beethoven identifies Leonore by means of the oboe—as Berlioz remarked in his article on *Fidelio*—Wagner develops the idea by using the oboe to characterize the femininity of Elsa, Elisabeth, Sieglinde, and the heroic Brünnhilde.[26] But most important, Wagner continues the Beethovian theme of human nature struggling against a hostile destiny and winning out through acts of feminine heroism.

From this point of view, the influence of *Fidelio* upon *The Flying Dutchman* seems especially significant to me. It is as if Wagner wrote his opera as a commentary upon Beethoven's. Where *Fidelio* presents us with an heroic female from the very start, *The Flying Dutchman* seeks to determine whether such a woman is possible, even to the mythic imagination. For countless ages the Dutchman has been circling the globe in the hope of encountering his Leonore, the woman whose fidelity will end his sufferings. When Senta accepts the role, she clothes herself in the hard masculinity of the "Yohohoe" Ballad, much as Leonore takes on male attire. The relationship between Senta and Erik duplicates the relationship between Marzelline and Jaquino. On the level of ordinary life, these are made for one another. But Senta's dedication to the Dutchman takes her beyond the world of Erik. She must, and does, prove that eternal fidelity is possible to woman. Though the

---

[24]The latter solution has been recommended by Paul Henry Lang, who suggests that the overture be used as a "grand postlude" or "recessional" (*Critic at the Opera* [New York: W. W. Norton, 1971], p. 109).

[25]On this it may be relevant to cite a conversation about the opera as quoted in a recent biography of Mahler: " 'You place *Fidelio* ahead of everything, even the works of Wagner?' Mahler asked. 'Yes, ahead of everything,' replied Förster. Mahler embraced him and said, 'We think alike' " (Henry-Louis de la Grange, *Mahler* [New York: Doubleday, 1973], I, 381).

[26]On this, see Maurice Kufferath, *Fidelio de L. Van Beethoven* (Paris: Librairie Fischbacher, 1913).

Dutchman has lost faith in her, she effects his salvation through a self-sacrifice that reminds us of Alceste as well as Leonore.

In the Dutchman himself one may also see an extension of Florestan, just as Captain Daland serves as a Rocco-like intermediary shuttling between the two levels of reality. Like his daughter Senta, who unifies the two levels, Captain Daland navigates between the mundane existence of the Norwegians and the ghostly being of the Dutchman's crew. The condemned Dutchman suffers, like Florestan, for no apparent crime. We never learn why Florestan has been thrown into prison except for the fact that he spoke the truth. Forces of evil, embodied in Pizarro, are taking vengeance upon him, but we learn nothing else about his case. Similarly, the Dutchman has fallen into the devil's hands just because he swore that he would not give up while fighting a storm at sea. He has done nothing wrong. He is merely the western male grappling with his destiny and being forced to suffer as a result. Like Florestan— and for that matter, the Don Giovannis in nineteenth-century literature—he can be saved only by a woman.

But not just *any* woman, as Leporello might have said. She must be a *faithful* one. In its emphasis upon the fidelity of the woman, the Wagnerian myth reverberates with a familiar ambiguity. In part, it implies that a faithful woman is so rare as to be a wonder in herself. In part, however, it also suggests that women are the only ones *capable* of approaching the ideal of fidelity, and therefore the only human beings who can provide salvation for the male adventurer. It is this idea that Nietzsche attacks in his criticism of the opera: "*The Flying Dutchman* preaches the sublime doctrine that woman makes even the most restless man stable; in Wagnerian terms, she 'redeems' him. Here we permit ourselves a question. Supposing this were true, would it also be desirable?" Nietzsche answers in the negative; it is better not to find one's Leonore: "The danger for artists, for geniuses—and who else is the 'Wandering Jew'?—is woman: adoring women confront them with corruption. Hardly any of them have character enough not to be corrupted.... Man is a coward, confronted with the Eternal Feminine—and the females know it."[27]

In a sense, Wagner agrees with Nietzsche. For the adoration of Senta does not bring happiness either to herself or to the Dutch-

[27]*The Case of Wagner,* trans. Walter Kaufmann (New York: Vintage Books, 1967), p. 161.

man. If it were happiness she sought, she would have married Erik. Instead, she saves the Dutchman by *removing* him from life. Throughout the opera, Wagner contrasts *die Liebe* ("love") with *die Treue* ("faith"). Senta feels the former towards Erik, the latter towards the Dutchman. Only he elicits what is called "eternal devotion," a oneness that transcends conjugal love in belonging to a deeper reality. Dying as she does, Senta proves her fidelity, destroys the curse, and allows the Dutchman and his crew to end their wanderings. This act of female heroism enables the couple to be reunited in the eternity of an afterlife. But it is only in death and through an end of what we call living that either hero or heroine can solve their problems.

Compared to this, Beethoven's solution is benign and even simple-minded. His work is always oriented to life, and even the music for *Egmont*—which ends with the protagonist dying as a political martyr—emphasizes the goodness of living heroically rather than the mystical benefits of dying. Imprisoned in Plato's cave, Florestan yearns for nothing but the world of sunshine. In Wagner, the cave signifies a sinful condition (as in *Tannhäuser*) that cannot be cured through any aspect of nature. If one reads *The Flying Dutchman* from a Lutheran perspective, one might even say that the Dutchman suffers from his human nature itself, from the original sin of striving without faith, of refusing to let God's grace sustain his being, of relying upon his own will instead of submitting to a higher love. This would be the secret sacrilege embodied in his oath against the storm. Senta then liberates him by taking his sinfulness upon herself through a Christ-like act of self-sacrifice.

Nothing comparable applies to Leonore and Florestan. He has been imprisoned unjustly, for no fault of any sort. If there is an original sin at the base of his suffering, it resides in the cruelty of repressive institutions. Leonore makes sacrifices to save him, but she does not sacrifice herself. Wagner wished to liberate men from the restless striving that belongs to material existence; Beethoven wished to liberate them from corrupt government and selfish or sadistic rulers. Though he composed music that is quasi-religious, Beethoven insists upon a humanistic ritual. He has none of Wagner's romantic mysticism, as he has none of his sentimentality. When Moscheles had finished the transcription of *Fidelio* and written "Finished, by the grace of God," Beethoven angrily scribbled the words "Man, help thyself."[28] His faith in mankind was for him

[28]Quoted in James, *Beethoven and Human Destiny*, p. 129.

what the love of God was for the medieval Christians. Wagner had neither the one nor the other. One often feels that only the nothingness of death could serve as his divinity.

Beethoven would not have understood the Wagnerian attitude. For all the bitterness that struggling entails, he saw no glory in escaping from life. Pizarro offers Florestan and Leonore the opportunity to die in each other's arms, much as Tristan and Isolde do in Wagner's opera. Beethoven's lovers refuse to take that way out. Tristan and Isolde have no world to keep them alive; they exist in no society and have no purpose beyond themselves. Florestan and Leonore survive *because* of the work they do. They believe in life and wish to contribute to it. They are, in fact, life itself, overcoming obstacles with joy and boundless energy. No one in music, or in any of the other arts, has expressed this ideal of human revitalization better than the Beethoven of *Fidelio*.

4. The Influence of Schiller

Fidelio was first performed in 1805. In that year Friedrich Schiller died. Though Beethoven never set Schiller's dramas to music, he saw the world as Schiller did and was surely influenced by his philosophical writings. Both men presuppose the Kantian dualism between a world of phenomena given in sense experience and that ultimate realm of noumenal being which reason and morality must posit even though it is unknowable. But both also deviate from Kant in treating art as an epiphany of the noumenal *within* the phenomenal. Where Kant had limited the aesthetic to the subjectivity of human responses, Schiller insisted upon a transcendental function that would give it the same kind of objectivity that Kant accorded the moral sense. It was in this Schillerian vein that Beethoven could say that "music is the only entrance to the higher world of knowledge which, though it embraces me, a man cannot grasp. . . . like all the arts, music is founded upon the exalted symbols of the moral sense: all true invention is a moral progress."[29]

For Schiller as well as Kant, it is pure and absolute freedom that characterizes man's reality, providing his ultimate capacity for the moral life as well as his destiny as a human being. In his essay "On the Sublime" Schiller explains man's misery by the fact that his

[29]*Beethoven: Letters, Journals and Conversations*, p. 76.

powers cannot be great enough to attain freedom in every aspect of his being. "All other objects obey necessity; man is the being who wills," he says, but then reminds us that nature imposes necessities upon man that he cannot will out of existence. In his struggle for freedom, man must therefore withdraw his allegiance from the coercion that reality imposes upon him. In Schiller's words, he must *"annihilate* as an *idea* the violence he is obliged to suffer in fact." Through moral education, man achieves this freedom from forces that subjugate him physically; and he is aided in this endeavour by an aesthetic faculty which Schiller analyzes into the beautiful and the sublime. In doing so, he resorts once again to Kant's distinction between the world of sense and the world of reason, but he tries to show how beauty and the sublime each presupposes that absolute freedom which is definitive of man's nature: "In the presence of beauty, we feel ourselves free, because the sensory instincts are in harmony with the laws of reason. In the presence of the sublime, we feel ourselves sublime, because the sensory instincts have no influence over the jurisdiction of reason, because it is then the pure spirit that acts in us as if it were not absolutely subject to any other laws than its own."[30]

These ideas are worth considering because they provide a conceptual framework that fits the temperament and the music of Beethoven. As if he had him in mind, Schiller tells us that the sense of the sublime is always a mixed feeling: at once painful, because based upon a recognition of physical debility, and joyous, even rapturous, in asserting its independence from the constraining laws of nature. When Schiller says, "Let him who cannot believe enjoy; he who can believe may renounce,"[31] he seems to be speaking directly to Beethoven. And it could very well have been Beethoven rather than Schiller who said: "Whatever I am I have become through an often unnatural tensing of my powers."[32]

This unnatural tensing Schiller explains by reference to the inevitable conflict between the real and the ideal, which he interprets as the conflict between the sensory and the rational. Having propensities for both, man is caught within a power struggle as

[30]*Complete Works of Friedrich Schiller in Eight Volumes* (New York: P. F. Collier & Sons, 1902), VIII, 139. This edition uses the word "sensuous" rather than "sensory," but I have made the change in order not to confuse Schiller's terminology with my own.

[31]Quoted in Thomas Mann, *Last Essays* (London: Secker and Warburg, 1959), p. 20.

[32]Ibid., p. 74.

BEETHOVEN: THE PASSION IN FIDELIO

each tries to dominate the other. Unlike Kant, Schiller refuses to bring peace through the easy submission of the sensory. He wishes to achieve an authentic harmony in which both aspects can flourish. That becomes the goal for his dramas as well as the *Kallias* letters and the *Letters on the Aesthetic Education of Man*. His theatrical works deal not only with man's failure to satisfy his ideals, but also with the need to accept the sensory phenomena which cause him to fail. The stress and the turmoil in the human condition as Schiller sees it come from man's search for a harmony that each of the two components desperately opposes. And if this is so, can one really believe in harmonization as a human possibility? Schiller, at least, is never sure; and into the dialectical structure of his thinking—the real or sensory in conflict with the ideal or rational—he always introduces uncertainty about harmonization itself. As ideals will always appear illusory to those who believe in the real, so too will the notion of harmonization seem like an illusion to one who is as sensitive to the reality of moral conflicts as Schiller was.

It is precisely this kind of sensitivity that Beethoven shares with him. Neither had the devotion to the sensuous that Goethe had, nor his assurance that reasonable ideals could lead man to a harmonious solution for his problems. The dynamism in Beethoven's music comes from more than just the struggle against external forces. One also feels that Beethoven is struggling against himself, even as a musician. He often seems to be fighting the very medium in which he writes, since music must always be sound and therefore an instance of the sensory world that ideal rationality wishes to overcome. At the same time, he rejects all ideals, sublime as they may be, that could dare to exclude the immediate pleasures of music. It is worth noting that improvisation came easily for him, music flowing out with a spontaneity that astounded the listeners. Only composition was painful and laborious. Is it too much to suggest that when he composed (and was therefore "serious" about his art), Beethoven felt the oppressiveness of his own aesthetic and moral ideals? In him as in Schiller, passion is generated not only by the attempt to go beyond the sensuous but also by doubts about the desirability of doing so.

As Jung also remarks, when Schiller talks about the real, he usually limits it to sensations and rarely mentions strong feelings or emotions.[33] Yet his plays and verses are extremely passionate in the

[33]C. G. Jung, "Schiller's Ideas upon the Type Problem," in *Psychological Types* (London: Kegan Paul, Trench, Trubner, 1946), pp. 87–169.

situations they depict and in their use of language. For violent conflict creates passion, which thrives on the need to overcome frustrating obstacles. In Schiller and Beethoven alike, these result from an inability to accept *either* the sensuous *or* the repressive rationality that would transcend it. Throughout their creative lives, both men oscillate between the two, as they also oscillate between belief and disbelief in the possibility of harmonization.

At the same time, Beethoven in his music and Schiller in his poetry resolve their problems by the fact of creativity alone. Though their works are tense and troubled, they are still harmonious in their ability to present the passionate struggles in a highly aesthetic manner. For them the painfulness of self-division becomes a phenomenon they surmount through the greatness of their art. Their striving for pure ideals serves as the theme of all their works; but their ability to express it in music and poetry already manifests a harmonization with sensuous reality. Their genius consists in the maximum exploitation of this paradox.

In other ways, too, Schiller prepares us for Beethoven. In his play about Joan of Arc, *The Maid of Orleans*, Schiller creates an heroic female not too different from Leonore. Schiller originally intended the work as a libretto or operatic poem, and in a letter to Goethe he writes: "I have always trusted that out of opera, as out of the choruses of the ancient festival of Bacchus, tragedy would liberate itself and develop in a nobler form. In opera, servile imitation of nature is dispensed with, and although this is allowed only as a special concession to operatic needs, here is nevertheless the avenue by which the ideal can steal its way back into the theatre."[34] *Fidelio* realizes this aspiration, just as the Choral Symphony creates through harmonious music that Elysium which Schiller sought as the aesthetic state man might someday attain on earth. Having no faith in a mystical love-death, Schiller had no other goal for that love of humanity which he poeticized and dramatized and conceptually handed on to Beethoven.

5. The Dangers of Idealism

In following Schiller and using his art to express conflict harmoniously, Beethoven inherits the artistic dangers of Schillerian

[34]Quoted in Mann, *Last Essays*, p. 56.

philosophy. Since harmony wins out through the mere existence of the aesthetic state, the real (which must always be inharmonious in itself) is never allowed to compete fully with the ideal. Their harmonization is always and ultimately of a sort that favors the ideal. Thus, in *Fidelio* the two levels of mythic being are so arranged that the bourgeois comedy expresses the real while passion leads us into the penetrating melodrama of the ideal. In being a singspiel, the work combines speech with singing, but in a hierarchy of importance. The spoken words suffice for reality; only the ideal merits the grandeur of Beethoven's music. Even where the real elicits music from Beethoven, that music is generally inferior to the rest. When Marzelline sings of her love for Fidelio, Beethoven gives her a pretty tune of no great musical interest. He obviously wishes to contrast her minor capacity for love with the enormous potentials of a Leonore. Mozart would have conveyed the same idea, as he does for the lesser characters in *The Abduction* and *The Magic Flute*, by writing sensuous music that indicates the exact configuration of Marzelline's love. It would not be inferior music, only music of a different sort.

Respecting the real and the sensuous as little as he does, Beethoven lacks this versatility. On one of the occasions when he said that *Figaro* and *Don Giovanni* were "repugnant" to him and "too frivolous" for his taste, Beethoven remarked that an opera he could write would have to be something he approached with "sincerity and love." But clearly these sentiments did not encompass every element in the opera. Though Beethoven can be magnificent in a military march when it pertains to some ideal activity, as in the stirring music of *Egmont* or even the happy village band passage in the Ninth Symphony, he seems insensitive to the dramatic possibilities of the prison guards' march in *Fidelio*. He cannot make it heroic, or even melancholy, for it is too brutish in its prison reality; and so he ends up with a grayish compromise.

At times, this disdain for the real leads Beethoven into the most felicitous of musical effects. The trumpet call at the climax in the dungeon is utterly unrealistic but wholly successful. It is the signal announcing the arrival of Don Fernando. But coming at the moment of Leonore's victory, which it also assures, Beethoven rightly magnifies the signal into a triumphant fanfare. Then he repeats it, like a rooster crowing a second time. In the opera and in the Leonore Overture Number 3, the extended trumpeting expresses the joyfulness of striving for an ideal as nothing else could possibly have done.[35] At other times, however, Beethoven tampers with the real less successfully. When Rocco tries to justify his leniency towards the prisoners by telling Pizarro that this is the king's birthday, we get a bit of iconography that sounds rather unconvincing. The music is somewhat kingly, but neither realistic nor idealized with great imagination.

In saying that Beethoven subordinates the real to the ideal, and the sensuous to the passionate, I do not mean to suggest that some other harmonization would have been preferable. For *him* to have written music, nothing else may have been possible. But approaching his work in this way, we may be able to understand its human import better than we could have otherwise. It may also help us to understand the basis of Tolstoy's attack on Beethoven. *The Kreutzer Sonata* reviles Beethoven's music as the expression of an idealistic love which Tolstoy considered delusion bordering on madness: "They say this music exalts the soul. Nonsense, it is not true! It has an effect, an awful effect—I am speaking of myself— but not of an exalting kind. It has neither an exalting or a debasing effect but it produces agitation."

For Tolstoy as well as the novel's narrator, romantic music— Beethoven's in particular—is a diabolical screen for erotic excitement. It pretends to some noble idealism while really arousing genital impulses and violent animality.[36] If this is true, the real has taken its revenge, as Freud insisted that it always does. However hard he might struggle in his music, Beethoven would still be striving for a sexual rather than a spiritual culmination. And, indeed, during the same conversation in which he says that music is the only entrance to "the higher world of knowledge," Beethoven also talks about it in language that sounds strongly libidinal: "Melody! I pursue her, I clasp her with new fire, she slips from me, is lost in the midst of vague impressions. Soon, driven by surging passions, I seize her again. I cannot loose myself from her, I must perpetuate her in a spasm of ecstasy with every urge of soul and body. And then, at the last, I triumph over her, I possess her whom I have pursued, for whom I have longed. And behold—a symphony."[37]

[35]This is not to say that the trumpet calls have an identical effect in the opera and in this overture. For interesting differences, see Martin Cooper, *Ideas and Music* (London: Barrie & Rockliff, 1965), pp. 11, 49.

[36]In a similar vein, the Chinese Music Institute of the May 7 Central Arts Academy denounced Beethoven in 1974 as a decadent "capitalist composer" whose music expresses *unhealthy* attitudes.

[37]Quoted in Rolland, *Goethe and Beethoven*, p. 5. These remarks of Beethoven were recorded by Bettina Brentano. She claims to have shown them to Beethoven

Beethoven then speaks of music as "the mediator between the life of the senses and the life of the spirit"; but skeptics may always wonder about the spiritualistic ingredient within this mediation.

Are we to conclude, then, that Beethoven is not only deficient in his appreciation of the sensuous, but also an unreliable guide to the nature of passion? In one of his letters he says that emotion is only for women and that music must burst as a flame from the mind of men.[38] Are we to take this as a deep self-deception, since Beethoven puts so much of his own emotion into his flamelike music? At various times Beethoven admits that he finds it extremely difficult to write for the human voice. Shall we infer from this that he was deaf to other people, and that only a composer who can appreciate the differences among men or women will know how to express *per musica* the variations in human affect?[39]

Even if we answered yes to these questions, we would scarcely jeopardize the greatness of Beethoven. We would merely conclude that his genius directed him towards other goals. He wished to inspire mankind, to fill it with his own driving energy, to lead it into a unifying fervor. It is only at this level that his achievement can fully and finally be understood.

6. The Passionate Remains

In the long essay on Schiller that he wrote towards the end of his life, Thomas Mann quotes, as follows, a passage in which Carlyle criticizes Schiller's humanitarian ideals: "We require individuality in our attachments. The sympathy which is expanded over all men will commonly be found so much attenuated by the process, but it cannot be effective on any. . . . Universal love of mankind forms but a precarious and very powerless rule of conduct. . . . The enthusiasm which pervades [Schiller's historical works,] elevated,

---

the following day, but it is possible that she eroticized them in the process of transcription.

[38]August 15, 1812. In *The Portable Romantic Reader*, ed. Howard E. Hugo, (New York: Viking Press, 1960), p. 606.

[39]On this, see Paul Bekker, *The Changing Opera* (New York: W. W. Norton, 1935), where it is argued that Beethoven's interest in ideas rather than in the individual singing voice makes *Fidelio* "the greatest example of the impossibility of approaching the theatre from a non-theatrical standpoint" (p. 85). As against this "old-stager" way of thinking about *Fidelio*, cf. Donald Francis Tovey, *Essays in Musical Analysis* (London: Oxford University Press, 1937), IV, 28–31, and V, 185–86, and George R. Marek, *Opera as Theater* (New York: Harper and Row, 1962), pp. 80–101.

strong, enlightened, would have told better on our hearts had it been confined within a narrower space."[40] Mann himself agrees with Schiller. He finds in Carlyle's attitude the dominant note of a nineteenth-century nationalism which still threatens the human race. In Schiller's appeal for a universal love of mankind Mann finds the only remaining hope for the world we live in.

Nietzsche scornfully called Schiller "a moral trumpeter," and others in the nineteenth century attacked him for "sentimentalizing history with so much false idealism."[41] Can a similar complaint be made against Beethoven? Or would Mann's defense of Schiller apply to him as well? The adulation that Beethoven enjoyed in the concert halls of Europe and America for at least a hundred years after his death was certainly related to the fact that he expressed a sense of humanitarian enthusiasm that mattered to millions of people. Did this make them politically more responsible or less so? Did Beethoven's works further the love of mankind or did they merely fabricate a passion that could only dissipate once the music ended?

To answer such questions, we would have to know more about human nature in these areas of aesthetics than we currently do. We can be sure that during the Second World War the opening bars of the Fifth Symphony did not serve merely as a conventional signal. They crystallized and distilled everything that Beethoven had said musically in works like *Egmont* and *Fidelio* about resisting tyranny. But the Nazis also used Beethoven's music for purposes of propaganda. To the present generation, it may no longer seem revolutionary: the elysium of the future has largely lost its appeal. Only as a masterful work of art, synthesizing the sensuous and the passionate within the musical dimensions of a politico-religious myth, is *Fidelio* sure to survive. This may not be as much as Beethoven had hoped for. It is nevertheless a great deal.

[40]Mann, *Last Essays*, pp. 92–93.
[41]Quoted in Erich Heller, *The Artist's Journey into the Interior, and Other Essays* (New York: Vintage Books, 1968), p. 61.

Index

153